# Table of Contents

WITHDRAWN FROM WORTH LIBRARY

**Introduction** ..................................................................7

## Chapter 1
**Asking the Right Questions** ..............................................9

Competency and Fit ...........................................................10
Key Competencies ............................................................11

## Chapter 2
**Interviewing from the Beginning** .................................15

Start the Interview Off Right ............................................18
Explanation of the Interview Process ..............................19
Get-to-Know-You Questions ............................................20
Work History ......................................................................21
Why This Job? ....................................................................22
Scholastic Experience .......................................................23
Job Performance ................................................................25
Career Objectives ..............................................................26
Self-Evaluation ..................................................................27
Managing Others................................................................28
Application: Starting the Interview Off Right ..................30
Building the Interview Questions .....................................36
Probes .................................................................................37

## Chapter 3
**Competency Questions** .....................................................43

Communication ..................................................................43
Interview Questions for Assessing Written
    Communication .............................................................46
Interview Questions for Assessing Verbal
    Communication .............................................................49
Interview Questions for Assessing Presentation Skills ......58
Application: Communication Skills Questions....................61

## Chapter 4
### Interpersonal Skills/Conflict Resolution ....................65

Interview Questions for Assessing Interpersonal Skills ....65

Interview Questions for Assessing Conflict-Resolution
Skills .............................................................................77

Application: Interpersonal/Conflict-Resolution
Skills Questions ...........................................................83

## Chapter 5
### Empathy and Service Orientation ................................89

Interview Questions for Assessing Empathy .....................90

Interview Questions for Assessing Service Orientation ....95

Application: Empathy/Service-Orientation Skills
Questions ...................................................................101

## Chapter 6
### Problem Solving................................................................105

Interview Questions for Assessing Problem-Solving
Skills ...........................................................................106

Application: Problem-Solving Skills Questions.................115

## Chapter 7
### Analytical Ability ............................................................121

Interview Questions for Assessing Analytical Skills ........122

Application: Analytical Skills Questions ..........................130

## Chapter 8
### Decision Making ..............................................................135

Interview Questions for Assessing Decision-Making
Skills ...........................................................................137

Application: Decision-Making Skills Questions ..............144

## Chapter 9
### Teamwork ..........................................................................147

Interview Questions for Assessing Teamwork Skills ........148
Application: Teamwork Skills Questions ..........................156

## Chapter 10
**Organization** ................................................................161

Interview Questions for Assessing Organization Skills ....162
Application: Organization Skills Questions ......................171

## Chapter 11
**Motivation**..................................................................175

Interview Questions for Assessing Motivation.................176
Application: Motivation Questions...................................185

## Chapter 12
**Initiative** ....................................................................191

Interview Questions for Assessing Initiative ...................192
Application: Initiative Questions .....................................198

## Chapter 13
**Stress Management** ........................................................205

Interview Questions for Assessing Stress-Management
    Skills ..................................................................206
Application: Stress-Management Skills Questions ............212

## Chapter 14
**Summary of Interview Tips** ...........................................215

## Chapter 15
**Other Competencies** .......................................................219

Ethics and Integrity ........................................................219
Ethics and Integrity Questions........................................220

## Chapter 16
### Work Ethics and Professionalism ...............................225
Work Ethics and Professionalism Questions ...............226

## Chapter 17
### Compliance ................................................231
Compliance Questions ...................................231

## Chapter 18
### daptability ..............................................235
daptability Questions ...................................236

## Chapter 19
### Leadership.................................................241
Leadership Questions ....................................242

## Chapter 20
### Creativity...............................................249
Creativity Questions ......................................250

## Chapter 21
### Skill-Based Behavioral Questions ...........................255

## Chapter 22
### Final Words......................................................273

## Chapter 23
### Summary List of Competencies...................................275

# Introduction

Interviewing potential employees is one of the most difficult and intimidating tasks a manager or business owner will ever face. The task is made even more daunting by the fact that repercussions of a poor hiring decision can haunt the employees, management and the company for a long time to come, and can potentially cost a great deal of money. Discovering how to decrease the risk and maximize the predictive ability of interviews is key to successful hiring.

We're taught that preparedness is the key to dealing with most challenging and stress-inducing situations. When applying for a bank loan or talking to investors or pitching a big sale, we plan and prepare diligently, and the same should be done before interviewing. The problem is that in an interview situation, the interviewee is at least equally as nervous, and usually even more so, than the interviewer. This lethal combination of nervous tension often negates even the most diligent planning and leaves the interviewer with very little information on which to base a solid recommendation.

It is so easy for an interview to become little more than a conversation. I'm not suggesting you want the interview to come off as an interrogation either, but what you need is for the information gained from the dialogue to be useful for, and relevant to, making a hiring decision. This means going beyond deciding what questions to ask and actually giving thought to what kind of answers you are looking for. What response will indicate that the candidate is a good fit for the position and your company? Are there responses that are totally incompatible with your organization's goals, mission and values? How will you deal with and evaluate completely unexpected (outrageous or brilliant) answers?

If you've done a good job of pre-selecting candidates for the interview stage, then all of the interviewees should be capable of doing a good job. Choosing which one will do the best job for you is not easy. The person who gives all the "right" answers often gets the job, but if there is no consideration given to what the right answers for your organization are, then a savvy, well-coached interviewee may be chosen over a less polished but more appropriate one. What this book is designed to do is help you determine the best questions to ask and determine the best answers. Not the best answers from a candidate's standpoint (their motivation is simply to get the job), but the best answers for you; satisfying your motivation to hire the person with the best fit, period.

# 1

# Asking the Right Questions

A successful interview is one that provides unique insight into the ability and willingness of a candidate to do a good job for your company. That means that the interview has to go beyond assessing the technical competence to do the job and get to the real core of the issue—does the person as a whole suit our company: our culture, our values, our ethics, our personalities? Will the person fit in and become a valuable addition to the workplace by doing excellent work, while at the same time contributing to a healthy work environment?

To uncover the answers to those questions, what you have to assess are the person's core business and professional competencies. By the time a potential employee gets to the interview stage, he or she better have all the technical skills and abilities necessary, otherwise you are wasting your time. The interview is the place to analyze the so-called "soft" skills that are not easily amenable to testing. The absence or presence of these skills is what leads to the diagnosis of such common job maladies as poor interpersonal skills, an attitude problem, a personality conflict, unable to work in a team, poor communication skills, and problem with authority. Some individuals truly are difficult and hard to get along with, but most, if given the right environment, are very able to adapt and fit into a workplace that is right for them.

*Note: Companies are notorious for hiring based on skill and ability, and firing based on fit.*

## Competency and Fit

Companies are notorious for hiring based on skill and ability, and firing based on fit. Many interviewers make the mistake of equating knowledge, skills and ability (KSA) with competency. In fact, competency is more closely related to an individual's suitability to the workplace than their actual education and experience. If you're hiring for a graphic artist, candidates can be easily eliminated based on their education, experience and portfolio of work. These factors are prerequisites for developing competency, but none of them (alone or in combination) can ensure that the candidate will indeed perform the job at the level you deem suitable. The final component in determining competency is the fit factor, and the best way to evaluate a candidate's overall competency is to screen for skill and ability and interview for competency and fit.

In practical terms this means limiting interview questions that are technical in nature and focusing more on questions that reveal a candidate's true character. Challenging questions, ones that make the applicant really self-assess, and even a few strategically placed, unexpected questions that throw the candidate off-guard, are the best types of questions for determining overall competency and fit. The interview should not be set up to be an intimidating interrogation, but it needs to be different enough that the even best-coached applicant has to stop and think and give an answer that is not anticipated or rehearsed. Remember, once the hiring decision is made, the interview façade is removed and the new employee with all of his or her innate characteristics, reactions and behaviors is unleashed in your workplace: you owe it to yourself and your current employees to figure out who this person is and what makes him tick before adding him to your team.

## Key Competencies

The entire list of competencies for any job will, of course, be different according to the job itself and the level of responsibility. A plumber must have expert plumbing skills whereas a computer programmer does not, but they both need to be able to communicate well and handle stress appropriately. The key competencies presented in this book are a compilation of the most common skills required to be successful on the job. Not every job will need all the competencies but most jobs will require most competencies. The specific areas of competence addressed in this book are:

- Communication

- People/Interpersonal skills

- Sociability

- Conflict resolution

- Decision making

- Team-building

- Organization

- Judgment

- Adaptability

- Motivation

- Initiative

- Compliance

- Stress management

- Leadership

- Analytical ability

- Creativity

- Integrity

It is up to each individual employer to assess the job and decide which competencies related to work habits and personal effectiveness are required for success in the position. Once that list has been established, it is time to turn your attention to developing questions that address each competency. At the same time you must learn how to ask the question and probe for details when required and construct an idea of the answer that is "right" for you, your team and your company. A candidate's fit can then be fairly and adequately assessed, and you should have a clear idea of who can and will do an excellent job for you.

*Interviewing at its best is a structured conversation.*

# 2

# Interviewing from the Beginning

Interviewing is intimidating for all parties. The interviewer wants to present a positive image of the company, and the interviewee wants to present their "best self" in hopes of being offered the job. This nervous tension provides the perfect environment for false impressions and social niceties when what you really need in an interview is a real conversation with a real person. That way both parties can assess whether or not there is a good fit and how likely it is that an employment relationship will be successful.

Interviewing at its best is a structured conversation. The interviewer is in control of how the conversation will flow, and the interviewee determines the actual content of the conversation through his or her responses to questions and probes. An ineffective interview is one that deteriorates into an impromptu conversation. While having a good ol' chat with someone is a way to pass the time, it is not going to reveal anything other than what the interviewee wants to reveal: usually a false impression. Basing hiring decisions on a "gut-feel" approach is the most common source of grievous hiring mistakes, and this approach needs to be avoided at all costs.

From the moment the candidate walks in the door to the moment he or she leaves, the interview needs to follow a set, but somewhat flexible, script. From the introductions to the question-and-answer period to the final good-bye, the interviewer must remain in control, and the best way to ensure that is through planning and preparedness. This is not to imply you should deliver interview questions like a robot or read from your piece of paper with hardly a glance at the person; the intention is to make the interview a smooth and objective process, facilitating a natural conversation within predetermined boundaries. This way the interviewer gains the information he or she needs, and the interviewee's responses can be compared to other candidates' responses quite easily.

A well-structured interview follows the same basic format:

- Introductions
- Small talk
- Explanation of the interview process
- Get-to-know-you questions
- Behavioral-based questions—assess competencies

- Interviewee asks questions

- Next steps

- Thank you and good-bye

It is important to begin the interview with some small talk, an explanation of the interview process, and some ice-breaker-type questions. This sets everyone at ease and prepares the candidate for what is to come. Remember, the objective of the interview is not to intimidate the candidate or set up the person for failure; you want to create an environment where the person can demonstrate to you whether or not he or she can do the job. For the interviewee to be able to do this, he or she must be relaxed. Unless you are recruiting for a position that requires nerves of steel, placing a candidate under undue stress and pressure will only elicit pressured responses. If you rely on this type of approach, you run the substantial risk of eliminating the more qualified person simply because of a difference in their ability to tolerate stress.

You're nervous, the candidate's nervous, but you have the ability to break the tension and set the stage for an informative and insightful discussion where the candidate can showcase his or her unique qualifications and you can assess whether or not the profile presented is a good fit for your company.

Organization and planning will get you 90 percent of the way—add some spontaneity and a genuine interest in getting to know the person sitting in front of you, and you have the perfect foundation for a meaningful and effective interview.

## Start the Interview Off Right

Your job as the interviewer is to lay the groundwork for an open, honest exchange of information. One of the best techniques for doing this is to start the interview off on a positive note. Set the interviewee at ease and ask questions that they are expecting and for which they will likely have fairly well prepared answers. When a candidate realizes that you are not trying to deliberately fluster them or catch them off-guard, they are more likely to let their guard down and give you answers that reflect their true person rather than the person they want to project in the interview.

Although your ultimate goal is to uncover the real person behind the interview façade, this is best accomplished by establishing rapport with the candidate. In this way you build trust and confidence, and you are in a much better position for discovering the individual's attitudes, beliefs and past patterns of performance. Ask the candidate to list their best qualities or tell you what factors they think are critical for success. The answers you get won't be particularly unique or insightful; they might not even be very truthful, but they will ensure the overall interview is effective and informative.

Remember, the insight value of opening questions is not intended to be high. The intention of these questions is simple: set the candidate at ease. A candidate who is confident with his or her responses at the beginning of the interview will likely remain confident in giving you honest and candid answers even as the questions become more probative and demanding. The end result is that you get progressively more relevant information as the interview progresses. Interviewing is a skill that requires patience, and as I'm sure you've heard, "good things come to those who wait!"

## Explanation of the Interview Process

Before beginning it is a good idea to prepare the candidate for what to expect. Make sure you cover the following:

- Small talk.

- Who is performing the interview.

- Necessary introductions.

- Discuss and explain behavioral questions.

- Talk about the interview process—who will be asking questions, time, next steps.

- Inform the candidate that you will be taking notes.

- Answer the candidate's questions.

At this point you are ready to begin the questions. You, the other interviewers and the candidate are prepared for what is to come. Stay focused, yet friendly, and remember your ultimate purpose is to get the answers you need to make an employment decision.

## Get-to-Know-You Questions

1.  Tell me about the hobby or activity you have participated in the longest.

2.  What are the first three things you do when you get up in the morning?

3.  What activities do you do in your spare time?

4.  What do you consider to be your greatest accomplishment?

5.  If you had to describe your major philosophy in life (without referring to any religion in particular), what would it be?

**Analysis:** The answers to these questions will give you a glimpse at what the interviewee values, or at least what he thinks you want him to value. For instance, if the candidate is intent on showcasing his or her education, the answers you get will likely emphasize academic performance or activity. The person might describe himself in terms of the degree or diploma he holds, or his greatest accomplishment may be a scholastic achievement. If the candidate focuses more on practical work experience, then he or she likely has more on a work record than on a school transcript. Still, other people may focus more on interpersonal skills and accomplishments.

The conversation will inevitably shift to the person's comfort zone and to the area of development in which he or she feels most confident. Make a note of the impression the candidate wants to give from the start and then make sure to probe fully into questions that deal with the areas not emphasized. The more well-rounded a person, the higher the chances of being able to deal with the changes and interpersonal skills required in most work environments.

## Work History

6. Tell me about the job you have right now.

7. What particular skills and abilities do you bring to your current job?

8. Does your current employer know you are actively seeking other work?

9. Can you give me a brief summary of your work history up to this point?

10. What have you accomplished in the past that makes you particularly qualified for this position?

11. Why are you leaving your current position?

**Analysis:** The main purpose for asking these questions is to get the candidate comfortable talking about their previous positions. You get information that goes beyond the traditional résumé list of responsibilities, giving you insight into the context of prior work. Gaining a better understanding of the person's prior work will help enormously when trying to make sense of the answers given to the behavioral questions ("Tell me about a time when...") that come later.

## Why This Job?

12. Why did you apply for this job?

13. How did you hear about this job opening?

14. What have you done to prepare for this interview?

15. What motivated you to be interested in this position?

16. This job is very different from your current position.

Tell me more about your choice to change the direction of your career.

**Analysis:** The answers to these questions are good to have, especially if you are torn between two or three outstanding candidates. Often the person who wants the position more will put in the extra time and energy necessary to be successful in a new position. If the person is venturing into a career change, knowing his or her motivation will help you judge the answer to specific behavioral questions even if the example is not industry relevant.

## Scholastic Experience

17. What was your favorite subject in school?

18. What was your best subject in school?

19. Why did you choose to major in _____?

20. What course gave you the most difficulty?

21. I see you attended college out of state. What was that experience like?

22. What courses have you taken that you feel best prepared you for this position?

23. What traits do you possess that made you a good student?

24. What traits do you possess that cause you to perform at a level below your potential?

**Analysis:** These questions are most suitable for recent graduates looking for their first job. They are also useful to set someone at ease who may not have a great deal of industry- or position-specific work experience. A person applying for his or her first supervisory job will gain confidence sharing course information that is particularly relevant, as will the person branching into a different career or one who upgraded his or her education.

When dealing with a recent graduate that has little previous work experience, the answers to the behavioral questions will come from educational experiences. It is important to understand his or her educational experience and the context in which he or she learned and performed well, and not so well. Although work is different than school, it still requires most of the same competencies: communication, teamwork, motivation, initiative, organization, etc.

## Job Performance

25. What kind of supervision do you think brings out the best in you?

26. Tell me about the supervisor with whom you got along the best.

27. Do you prefer to work alone or as part of a group?

28. What are some job responsibilities you do not like?

29. What aspects of your last job did you really like?

30. What is the most important element you require in a job?

**Analysis:** These questions set the foundation for future behavioral-based questions that deal with how the person performed on the job rather than just what duties they performed. Use these questions as practice for the more inquisitive and precise behavioral questions that assess a specific competency in depth. These questions simply ask the candidate to self-assess or give an opinion, but it gets him or her in the habit of thinking about a job in particular rather than work in general.

Some of these questions will also help you determine overall fit. There are times when a particular culture or style of supervision is obviously not going to work with a particular candidate. Rather than going through the entire interview, you have the option of cutting the process short if it is a clear mismatch from the beginning. Hopefully the pre-interview process has uncovered any glaring fit issues, but sometimes the rapport built during the early stages of the interview is enough to break through even the most heavily armored shell.

## Career Objectives

31. What is your long-term career objective?

32. Why have you decided to leave your past jobs?

33. How does this job fit with your overall career goals?

34. Where do you see this role taking you in the future?

35. What areas do you need to further develop in order to meet your career goals?

36. What specific events or activities in your past have most influenced your current career objectives?

**Analysis:** Study after study have proved that a satisfied employee is a productive employee, and one of the key elements of job satisfaction is a stimulating work environment. Not everyone who works for you will be promoted, but building a workforce that is enthused about and eager to take on extra assignments and responsibility creates a very dynamic and productive environment. People who have already set goals for their career will be much more amenable to setting goals for on-the-job results, and these are the type of people who will contribute the most to your company. Employee selection is a costly function, and doing it right the first time will save a great deal of time and money in the long run. Hiring employees who are interested in, and capable of, contributing a wide range of skills and talents to your workplace are the ones who have the greatest long-term potential.

## Self-Evaluation

37. As an employee, how do you describe yourself?

38. How would your last supervisor describe you?

39. How would your coworkers describe you?

40. In what type of job-related activity are you most confident performing?

41.   What has given you the most satisfaction at work?

42.   How do you know when you have done a good job?

43.   When you assess your performance, what factors do you use for your evaluation?

**Analysis:** These questions are purely opinion; questions meant to get the candidate used to opening up about their previous work performance. You'll be able to tell what behaviors and characteristics the person feels are critical for success; you won't be able to tell how well the person actually applies those behaviors and characteristics. The primary purpose of self-evaluation questions is to uncover which characteristics a candidate finds the most valuable. Whatever qualities the candidate focuses on are the ones that he or she believes are the most important to the position for which they are applying. Use the answers to gauge fit with the company's values.

## Managing Others

44.   What is your overall philosophy when managing or supervising others?

45.   How do you motivate others to perform their very best?

46. When evaluating the performance of a person who reports to you, what factors do you consider are the most important?

47. What do you do that sets an example for your employees and coworkers?

48. How would you describe your basic leadership style?

49. If I asked your employees to describe you, what would they say?

50. How frequently do you meet with your employees as a group?

**Analysis:** When interviewing for a management or supervisory position, it is crucial that you consider how well the person will fit with your current employees and what leadership philosophy to which the person ascribes. Different work environments and industries are more suited to some styles of leadership than others. What you need to know is what style the candidate is most comfortable with and what has given him or her the most success in the past. There are some very fair yet dictatorial managers who are considered good leaders by their people. Whether or not your people and your culture will see it that way is another story.

Throughout the getting-to-know-you phase of the interview, be aware of the applicant's poise, style of delivery and communication ability; these are all valuable clues to whether or not the person is suitable for the job and whether he or she will fit into the work environment.

## Application: Starting the Interview Off Right
### Applicant: Charles Davenport

### Position: Administrative Assistant

Interviewer: "Hello Charles, I'm Dianna. We spoke on the phone. I'm pleased to meet you in person. Were my directions okay?"

Interviewee: "Oh yes, I found the place with no problem."

Interviewer: "Great. I see you've met Carol our receptionist. I'll introduce you to others as we go. We're ready to get started so if you want to follow me, I'll show you to the boardroom."

Interviewee: "Sure."

Interviewer:     "I know we discussed the fact that two of us will be doing the interview. Don't worry, we're not here to intimidate you; we simply find it's very valuable to get more than one opinion on a person's suitability."

Interviewee:     "I understand, and I've been preparing for the interview."

Enter Boardroom

Interviewer:     "Charles, I'd like you to meet Greg. Greg is our Administration Manager and is the direct supervisor of the position for which you are applying. He and I will be conducting the interview together. The types of questions we'll be asking are mostly behavior-based questions. That means we are looking for you to describe a particular situation you have encountered in the past: what the situation was, what you did, what other people did, and what the outcome was. We're interested in discovering what you have actually done rather than what you think you would do in a given circumstance. Do you have any questions about this type of interview?"

Interviewee: "What happens if I can't give you an example from my past experience?"

Interviewer: "Well, the questions we ask in the interview process focus mostly on personal traits and characteristics rather than specific skills. If you haven't encountered a work situation that deals with the particular attribute we are discussing, the likelihood is very high that you've encountered it in another area of your life. Remember, Greg and I are not here to trick or confuse you; we need to get to know who you are and how you react in various situations in order for us to evaluate whether this job is a good fit for you and if you are a good fit for our organization.

"We're each going to take turns asking the questions, but please feel free to direct your responses to either of us and ask questions if you are unclear about anything as we progress. Also, silence does not bother us—we want you to give us a really good example of the characteristics we are talking about; if it takes you a moment to think of an example, that's okay. If you need some help, we'll try to rephrase the questions or jog your memory as best we can. Are you ready to get started?"

Interviewee:     "Sure, as ready as I'll ever be."

Interviewer:     "Oh, one last thing: In order for us to remember your responses we will be taking notes. Please don't let that distract you."

Interviewee:     "Okay."

Interviewer:     "Okay, let's start by having you telling us a bit more about yourself. Tell me something that I wouldn't know just from reviewing your résumé."

Interviewee:     "Well, I'm sort of an expert at BBQ. I took a course a while back and really enjoyed it so now I experiment with all different kinds of meats, vegetables and techniques, I've created my own marinades, and all my neighbors seem to pop in for a surprise visit just after I've lit the BBQ."

Interviewer:     "We'll just highlight your address at the top of your résumé! Thanks for sharing your special talent with us. Now, I see you are currently working in administration; can you tell me why you are applying for this job?" [The candidate demonstrated a willingness to share personal information so no further probing is needed. This is where you want to set the candidate at ease and develop rapport—his response indicates that the interviewer has done that.]

Interviewee: "Sure, I've been in my current role for three years and I really enjoy it but the company is small and there is very little room for advancement. I am really looking to establish a long-term career in a company where I can grow and develop my skills."

Interviewer: "So what is the most important element you require in a job?"

Interviewee: "What I require is the knowledge that my efforts will be rewarded with opportunities for career development. I get pay raises at my current job, but what I really want is the opportunity for more responsibility."

Interviewer: "How do you know when you've done a good job?"

Interviewee:      "I know when I do a good job because I feel like I did everything I could in the situation. I don't need someone else to be constantly telling me what a good job I did, although that's nice every so often. I can tell in myself when I've worked hard at a job and done my best."

Interviewer:      [Probe] "Tell me about a time when you knew you did an exceptional job and no one commented specifically on it."

Interviewee:      "Actually, it was just last week. It was our company's year-end and we were so busy. The accounting clerk was just run off her feet so I was slated to process the payroll and I only received my cross-training last month. I am proud to say that I got the payroll completed on time and error-free. I got confused a couple of times but I managed to work it out using the resources from the payroll company and without having to get the accounting clerk to do it for me."

The interview is underway and the candidate seems calm and relaxed. Now is the time to start asking competency-focused questions. These questions are behavioral-based and require specific examples for each answer. By building a comfortable interview environment, you are now in a prime position to get honest, straightforward answers that will help you determine whether or not the person sitting in front of you has the right mix of personal competencies and technical skills.

## Building the Interview Questions

The following chapters provide examples of questions designed to assess each of the core competencies recognized by most employers. While a well-rounded person may exhibit competence in most of the core areas, each position typically has four to six competency areas that are absolutely critical. Examine your job description and determine which areas require the greatest amount of attention. Think about what specific attributes will set one technically qualified candidate apart from another equally qualified candidate; by focusing on these distinguishing characteristics, the key competencies for the job will emerge.

Once you've determined which competencies you want to interview for, ask two or three of the questions per category. This will ensure adequate coverage of positive and negative examples that relate to the attribute, and it gives the candidate an opportunity to provide more detail and, often, another example. The answer guidelines are provided to give you an idea of what to look for and will also highlight what types of answers are better suited to particular cultures and work environments in general.

# Probes

Follow-up questions are designed to give you, the interviewer, more information about the situation being described. By asking questions, you will be able to get answers that you want and not just answers the candidate is most willing to provide. Often the candidate will stall during their explanation of an event, and probes from you help them stay focused and recall details they might have otherwise missed. Probes are also an excellent way to demonstrate effective listening. You can't "zone out" if you're listening for areas in the explanation that need more clarification or elaboration.

Examples of effective probes include:

WHY?

- Why did you decide to do that?

HOW?

- How did you feel?

- How did he or she react?

- How did you handle that?

- How did you resolve that?

- How did you prepare for that?

## WHEN?

- When did this happen?

## WHERE?

- Where were you when this happened?
- Where was your supervisor/coworker?

## TELL ME MORE

- Tell me more about your interaction with that person.

## CAN YOU GIVE ME AN EXAMPLE?

## LEAD ME THROUGH THE PROCESS.

## WHO

- Who else was involved?
- To whom did you report?

## WHAT

- What did you do?
- What did you say?
- What was your role?

- What steps did you take?

- What action did you take?

- What happened after that?

- What was your reaction?

- What was the outcome/result?

- Were you happy with that outcome/result?

- What do you wish you had done differently?

- What did you learn from that?

- What was your logic?

- What was your reasoning?

- What time was it?

- What was your role?

- What obstacles did you face?

- What were you thinking at that point?

When probing an applicant to expand on their answer, it is important that you don't lead the person to the "right" answer; good probes are simply a request to "tell me more." Try to avoid judging an answer or leading the candidate to the correct answer. Examples:

Question:         "How would your coworkers describe you?"

Answer:            "I think most of my coworkers would say I'm
                   pleasant and easy to get along with."

Judgment:          "So, when you work with teams you're the one
                   everyone still talks to when there is conflict?"

Answer:            "I suppose, I actually try to stay out of the
                   drama as much as possible."

Leading Probe:     "Working in a team environment would likely
                   be a good option for you?"

Answer:            "Oh yes, I love to work with other people."

Good Probe:        "Tell me more about the context of your
                   interactions with coworkers."

Answer:            "Well, I do most of my work alone in the back,
                   but we all go on break together and we get
                   along real well. It is a really great team
                   environment."

Notice that with the first two probes the interviewer assumed
that since the candidate reported being friendly and easy to get

along with, that he or she was also a good member in a team environment. The answers shed no light on the candidate's actual work performance, only reinforced the erroneous assumption that the candidate worked in a team environment. By asking a direct probe regarding the candidate's interaction with other coworkers, the interviewer is quickly able to determine that the person doesn't actually work in a team environment.

It is very easy to lead a candidate to the correct answer but it is often imperative that you get more information than the candidate originally offered. Don't be afraid to probe if you don't feel the answer gave you sufficient insight. Sometimes the candidate will continue to offer superficial answers, so you have to get used to rephrasing questions and asking for details until you are satisfied with the answer given.

*Effective communication for one person may be deemed ineffective by the other for no other reason than a difference in style.*

# 3
# Competency Questions

## Communication

We hear so much today about the importance of communication or the ability to communicate with others, both in written and verbal formats. The difficulty in assessing or evaluating communication is that it necessarily involves two people. Effective communication for one person may be deemed ineffective by the other for no other reason than a difference in style. Does that make one of the parties a better or worse communicator? Not necessarily: it depends on the context. For a person employed in a job that involves public speaking, his or her communication style must have broad appeal in order to be considered effective. For the research scientist working in the lab, effective communication will likely involve much less flamboyance, but a direct and to-the-point style is not necessarily ineffective. Effective communication is about sending and receiving messages, so it is important not to have an idea set in stone about what constitutes effective communication before evaluating the purpose of the communication required.

Being able to hear the message being sent is equally important to effective communication as being able to send a message. The second part of effective communication is, then, active listening. Listening for clues to discover the intent behind the communication is vital for deciding how to respond and, thus, completing the communication cycle. An interview is an excellent forum to evaluate both sides of the communication equation—it involves active listening and clear expression, and you should know by the end whether or not the individual sitting before you is an effective communicator.

Effective communication, regardless of the style, requires five skill areas:

## Asking questions

In order to fully understand a message being sent, and thus respond appropriately, a person must ask clarifying questions when necessary. Not asking questions will eventually lead to misunderstandings; the root cause of most communication breakdowns.

## Effective listening

For good communication to occur, the message receiver must listen attentively to the speaker and provide the speaker clues that he or she is being listened to. A simple nod of the head or affirmative response conveys to the speaker that their message is being heard and respected.

## Detecting inconsistencies

Taking information at face value is a potentially fatal mistake that many people make. The ability to detect and then question inconsistency is essential for effective communication. A message that is untruthful but well heard can cause more harm than plain ignorance of an accurate message.

## Paraphrasing/Summarizing

Active listening is the first step toward true understanding, but the best way to guarantee understanding is to summarize the points made by the speaker. The speaker then has the opportunity to make corrections, and both parties are secure in the knowledge that the message is clear.

## Maintaining contact

Okay, so you've exchanged a message with someone; now it is important to follow up. The discussion of an impending deadline and assigning tasks may be executed very effectively, but the only way to evaluate the final outcome of the communication is to maintain contact and keep current. Needs or circumstances may change, making follow-up critical to an effective communication cycle.

When asking a candidate questions that involve communication skills, it is wise to keep these five skill areas in mind. Evaluate the candidate's answer based on how well they demonstrate the appropriate skills and techniques in order to communicate effectively. Essentially, the entire interview provides clues about a person's ability to communicate. Does the applicant communicate effectively with you? Does he or she ask questions and paraphrase in order to fully understand what you are asking? In an interview situation, the candidate is nervous and, thus, he or she will likely use the same level of communication skills used on the job and in other stressful situations.

## Interview Questions for Assessing Written Communication

51. Tell me about a time in which you had to use your written communication skills in order to get an important point across.

**Analysis:** Use this question to assess whether or not the candidate understands when it is best to use written communication versus direct oral communication. In this day of e-mail and instant messages, it is extremely important for people to recognize the limitations of written communications and also know when it can be used most effectively.

52. Describe for me the last written communication you had with your boss.

**Analysis:** This question allows you to determine if the candidate recognizes when written communication is more appropriate than verbal communication. Not everything in the workplace needs to be done in writing, and no one has time to put everything in writing. Knowing in what circumstances a written memo or letter is required is key to working efficiently and communicating effectively.

53.  Describe the most significant written document, report or presentation that you worked on.

**Analysis:** To evaluate the extent of the applicant's written communication experience and expertise. Discovering the reaction to the written material is key to be able to determine level of skill.

54.  Tell me about one of the most important written documents you were required to complete. How did you determine when it was finished? What reaction did it receive?

**Analysis:** Written documents can be edited and revised forever. What this question is designed for is to understand if the candidate knows when a document covers what it needs to.

55.  Tell me about the best written proposal you have created. Why was it the best? How did you know that it was good?

**Analysis:** Ask this type of question if the ability to prepare and present written communication represents a significant skill for the job. Delve into why the document or presentation or proposal was so important and what the candidate contributed that was equally significant. Pay close attention to the external and internal cues the candidate used in order to evaluate the effectiveness of the communication. Candidates who rely mostly on intrinsic cues and rewards are more likely to produce high-quality work regardless of the circumstances, while those who need extrinsic responses usually need more coaxing to produce superior work.

56. Often the problem with written communication is that we never know if the person receiving the message followed up or took action. Can you give an example of a time when your written request was not acted upon? What did you do about it?

57. When have your verbal communications been important enough to follow up in writing?

**Analysis:** What you are looking for with this question is whether or not the individual follows up written communication with further contact. It is not enough to fire off memos and letters; the onus is on the person who initiates the communication to make sure his or her message was received. Answers that indicate the person has learned this important component of communication are desirable.

# Interview Questions for Assessing Verbal Communication

58. Discuss a time when you had to assert yourself (speak up) in order to get a point across that was important to you.

**Analysis:** Assertiveness is an important quality. A person may communicate very well when everyone is in agreement, but if he lacks the gumption to speak his mind and fears, creating dissention or conflict, then the person's usefulness as a team member is limited. It's also a fine line between assertion and aggression, and you need to ensure the candidate you choose clearly knows the difference.

59. Have you had to "sell" an idea to your coworkers, classmates or group? How did you do it? Did they "buy" it?

**Analysis:** In the world of work, the most common use of communication is to persuade someone to do something: buy something, sell something, complete something, do something correctly, etc. Listen carefully to what the person's example is, though; some people are very good at the "art of the sale," but if what they are selling is not useful, then the effort is wasted. Again, it is a fine line between persuasion and coercion, so do some extra probing if you suspect the person has a tendency toward the latter.

60. Give me an example of a time when you were able to successfully communicate with another person, even when that individual may not have personally liked you. How did you handle the situation? What obstacles or difficulties did you face? How did you deal with them?

**Analysis:** This question involves interpersonal communication, a competency that will be discussed in depth in the next chapter. However, the act of communication is about communicating with other people, and it is the most challenging when you are dealing with someone you don't like. What you are looking for in this answer is an acknowledgement that not all people are likeable but that the candidate can reign in his or her personal feelings for the sake of the company.

61. Describe a situation you were involved in that required a multi-dimensional communication strategy.

**Analysis:** This question is another way to determine if the candidate knows how to use written and verbal communication appropriately, and how well he or she combines the two mediums for maximum effect.

62. Give an example of a difficult or sensitive situation that required extensive communication.

**Analysis:** Sensitive situations call for highly effective communication skills. Clearly understanding the original message and then clearly articulating a response are imperative for the dialogue to be constructive. Communication at its best is open to so many opportunities for breakdown, so when the subject matter is highly sensitive, the communication must be as close to perfect as possible. Look for the effective use of listening, empathy and maintaining contact.

63. How do you ensure that someone understands what you are saying?

**Analysis:** The essence of this question is to learn if the candidate recognizes the importance of active listening and actually practices the skill.

64. Give me an example of a situation where proper communication allowed you to get the task/project done quickly.

65. Tell me about a time when the ability to communicate effectively was critical to the success of a task or project. How did you handle it?

66. Give me an example of a time when you had to explain a complicated procedure to someone who was new to

the situation. What did you do? What were the results?

67. Describe a recent situation when miscommunication created a problem on the job.

**Analysis:** Effective communication builds a foundation for efficiency. Ideally, the candidate will be able to give you an example that demonstrates his or her understanding of this relationship. When communication falters, it can cause significant lags in a project's completion. What you want to uncover is how the candidate handles communication breakdown: what are the signals, what does he or she do about it, how effective is the intervention, etc.

*Many high-energy individuals have a bad habit of not listening carefully.*

68. Tell me about a time when you really had to pay attention to what someone else was saying, actively seeking to understand their message.

69. Tell about a time when your active listening skills were critical to the success of a project.

70. Describe for me a situation where you missed some important details that were communicated to you. What was the outcome? How did you resolve the situation?

**Analysis:** Active listening is so important, and it contributes to effective communication as well as sets the stage for good interpersonal relationships. Many high-energy individuals have a bad habit of not listening carefully. These people get jobs done quickly and show a great deal of initiative and motivation, but they often misplace their energy. What you want to know is whether or not these enthusiastic types have learned from this mistake and recognize the importance of active listening.

71. Describe for me an instance when you jumped into a task or project before you fully understood the entire concept.

72. Discuss a situation where your failure to listen

attentively to a coworker or supervisor caused ill feelings because of their hastiness to get going before you fully understood what they were trying to communicate.

**Analysis:** Poor listening is one of easiest ways to create communication breakdown. Situation comedy writers rely on miscommunication for their source of humor. Fortunately, on TV, by the end of the thirty minutes the situation gets resolved. In the workplace it takes much longer and can cause a significant amount to damage to productivity and relationships. Ineffective listening happens all the time, so you want employees who understand this fact and have learned how to avoid it. Look for indications that the candidate summarizes and paraphrases by listening to the examples given, as well as the way he or she answers and clarifies questions.

73.  Describe a situation you observed or were a part of where you feel communication was handled particularly well by someone else. What did they do? Why do you think it was effective?

74.  Tell me about a time when you had difficulty understanding a conversation and the point the person was trying to make. What did you do? What was the final outcome?

75.  Give me an example of a time when you were unclear about the directions given to you for a work assignment. What did you do to clarify the directions? What was the final outcome?

**Analysis:** Good communication skills are often best learned in a practical setting. When a candidate can relay an example of communication, that is in fact representative of excellent communication, that is a strong indicator that he or she truly "gets" what good communication is. The reverse is also true: If a candidate knows first-hand how frustrating it is to be the one who does not understand, he or she will likely make a concerted effort to be understood when speaking.

76.  Tell me about a time when you worked with someone who was very difficult to understand. Perhaps the person's first language was not English or he had a disability that affected his ability to communicate. Explain how you overcame the situation.

**Analysis:** Workplaces today are multicultural and inclusive of people with varying degrees of ability. The likelihood that an employee will need to communicate with a customer or coworker who is hard to understand is very high. Use this question to discover what types of strategies the candidate employs in difficult situations. Does he or she mention body language and other non-verbal clues? Does the person recognize the power of paraphrasing, summarizing and asking questions? Probe the candidate about the outcome of the communication. Ask if he or she felt frustrated and how those feelings were handled.

77.  Tell me about how you communicate with your current supervisor concerning project process, concerns and suggestions.

78.  Your supervisor has given you instructions to complete a project. You are not clear as to some of the details of the instructions. What do you do?

79.  Describe for me the last conversation you had with a person in your organization that was senior to you but not a direct supervisor or manager.

**Analysis:** Communicating with supervisors is slightly different than with coworkers. There is a level of responsibility and authority that needs to be respected, and an astute interviewer uses this question to determine how much the candidate adjusts his or her communication as it goes up the organization chart. This is not to say that you want employees who are intimidated by, or scared of, talking to superiors. What you want are employees who recognize a reporting authority exists and make a concerted effort to keep the supervisor informed and advised as required.

80. Describe a situation when you were able to strengthen a relationship by communicating effectively. What made your communication effective?

81. Describe how your ability to communicate effectively and build relationships with many different types of people has contributed to one of your greatest accomplishments.

**Analysis:** These are general questions aimed at determining what factors the candidate considers essential to effective communication. There is no clue given as to what the interviewer thinks effective communication should entail, so the candidate must come up with his or her own definition. These are excellent opening questions for the topics of communication and interpersonal skills.

82. Describe some tough or tricky situations in which you had to talk to people to obtain information you needed to make an important decision or recommendation.

83. Walk me through a situation in which you had to obtain information by asking a lot of questions of several

people. How did you know what to ask?

**Analysis:** An element of active listening is the ability to ask enough questions to make sure you understand the message being sent. The key, though, is to ask enough of the right questions. Neither party wants to keep trying to make himself or herself understood, so an effective communicator gets to the point quickly and efficiently and avoids frustration.

## Interview Questions for Assessing Presentation Skills

84. Tell me about a time when you had to make a presentation to a large group.

85. Tell me about a time when you had to make a presentation to a small group.

86. What has been your experience with giving presentations to large or small groups?

87. Have you prepared and communicated ideas and information in a formal setting? Please explain.

88. Tell me about a time when you were required to give a presentation and it did not go as planned. What happened? What contributed to the problem? What would you do differently?

**Analysis:** While some jobs do not have a presentation requirement, it is a skill that is used in a wide variety of positions. While a receptionist or administrator may greet clients/customers, answer questions and present information informally, the position still requires confidence and poise. Similarly, when the safety inspector tours a facility, the production worker may be asked to demonstrate machinery or answer questions, again requiring basic presentation skills. Being able to present information coherently is not a requirement for self-confidence, but it is often co-relational. Confidence is usually exhibited by the most talented people, and those are the people you want working for you.

89. Tell me about a recent speech or presentation you gave that you consider successful. How did you know it was successful? How did you prepare? What obstacles did you face? How did you handle them?

90. What has been your most successful experience in speech-making?

91. Think about the last presentation you gave. Describe for me the supplementary materials you prepared and any other aids you used. How were these materials received by the audience?

**Analysis:** Presenting information well requires a great deal of time and preparation, and this type of question should be used to determine how much energy a candidate puts into the prep work. Some people think that by "winging it" they can present a balanced and professional presentation, but it usually comes across as haphazard and scattered. If formal presentations to various stakeholders are part of the job description, then be sure to probe for the details.

92. Tell me about a time when you had to present complex information.

93. Many jobs require us to give a formal, stand-up presentation. Tell me about the most challenging presentation of this type you ever had to make. What made it so challenging? How did you prepare for it? How did it turn out?

**Analysis:** Giving presentations is a highly specialized skill. Public speaking is stressful, and when the subject matter is complex or difficult to explain, the task is even more intimidating. This type of question allows the interviewer to determine what the candidate considers challenging and how he or she goes about including the audience in the presentation and facilitate learning or understanding. Probe to find out how the candidate measured the success of the presentation: did he or she give a quiz, provide follow-up, require feedback, etc.?

## Application: Communication Skills Questions
### Applicant: Charles Davenport

### Position: Administrative Assistant

Interviewer: "In the role as Administrative Assistant you will be required to assist the Sales Manager with presentations. Have you prepared and communicated ideas and information in a formal setting? Please explain."

Interviewee: "Yes, I have. In my last position I was very involved with helping my manager present new policies or procedures to the employees. One of the main projects I worked on was preparing a new policy and procedure manual, and I was in charge of preparing all the material needed to present the new information to the employees at the staff meeting. My manager gave the overview of the project, the rationale and process used, and I was responsible for the actual dissemination of specifics. What I did was prepare a PowerPoint presentation that had each of the new policies, and we went through the key changes one by one. Everyone had a chance to ask questions of both of us, and it was very well received."

Interviewer: "Tell me about how you communicate with

your current supervisor concerning project processes, concerns and suggestions."

Interviewee: "Well, I try to keep my boss very well informed. I work as her assistant so she needs to know where I am at with all my projects. We have an arrangement where I can come to her with any questions and concerns and she requires a daily update on my progress with long-term tasks."

Interviewer: "What about suggestions you may have? How do you communicate those ideas?"

Interviewee: "I try not to spring things on her. I think my ideas through, and then if they truly make sense, I ask for a meeting. That way I have time to prepare my suggestion, and I know she has time to hear what I am saying."

Interviewer: "Communication is often a key stumbling block for a project's success. Give me an example of a situation where proper communication allowed you to get a task/project done quickly."

Interviewee:     "That happened a few months ago. My boss
                 asked me to pull all the training records for the
                 staff. I knew that was a huge undertaking
                 because some of the records were in the
                 employee files, some in the personnel files and
                 some in the computer database. I asked her the
                 purpose for pulling the files and when she said
                 she needed it to determine if all the first-aid
                 certificates were up to date. When she said it,
                 we both realized that we had created a database
                 for that exact purpose last year when the last
                 group attended their re-certification. By asking
                 that one question, I saved a lot of time and got
                 the information to her within the hour."

Notice how the interviewer helps Charles understand the
relevance of the question being asked. Rather than just jumping
right in with the question, he provides some background
information about why the question is being asked. This sets
the candidate at ease and it also provides strong contextual
clues so the candidate can discuss an example that is both
applicable and appropriate. The key with providing these lead-
ins is to make sure you don't lead the candidate toward the
"right" answer. You shouldn't have to use these explanations
with every behavioral question, but it is a technique that often
saves time.

Charles did not appear to need many explanations, and his

answers to the communication questions were quite good. Certainly no red flags were raised, and the interviewer probed for more specific information regarding how the applicant actually used good communication to work efficiently.

*Use explanatory lead-ins to supplement your behavioral questions, making them relevant to your company and the position.*

# 4

# Interpersonal Skills/ Conflict Resolution

Interpersonal skills are the broad range of skills that allow people to communicate effectively, build rapport and relate well to all kinds of people. Listen for self-awareness, understanding and an ability to communicate effectively with others regardless of differences. Be sure to probe for as many details and specifics as possible, such as names, dates and other verifiable information. Skilled interviewers will also ask candidates for their thoughts or feelings about a situation to gain further insight.

## Interview Questions for Assessing Interpersonal Skills

94. Describe the types of people you get along with best and why.

95. How have you developed your interpersonal skills?

96. Describe your relationship with the people you work with.

97. Tell me about your relationship with a coworker whom you work well with.

**Analysis:** These are good openers for the interpersonal section. Use probes to get the details and ask for specific examples. What you are looking for is an understanding that although a person may not like a coworker, customer, boss, etc., he or she must develop coping mechanisms to ensure communication is clear and the work environment is pleasant. Often a person will get along best with someone who has a similar personality and outlook on life, so the answers to these questions can reveal quite a bit about the candidate's true self.

98. Describe the most difficult working relationship you've had with an individual. What specific actions did you take to improve the relationship? What was the outcome?

99. Describe the types of people you have difficulty getting along with and why.

100. Think about a difficult boss, professor or other person. What made him or her difficult? How did you

successfully interact with this person?

101. Tell me about your relationship with a coworker whom you do not have a good working relationship. What steps have you taken to improve that relationship?

102. Describe how you handle rude, difficult or impatient people.

103. Tell me about a time when you had to work with a difficult boss.

104. Tell me about the most difficult or frustrating individual that you've ever had to work with, and how you managed to work with them.

105. Describe a situation when you wished you'd acted differently with someone at work. What happened? What did you do about the situation?

106. Give an example of when you had to work with someone who was difficult to get along with. How/why was this person difficult? How did you handle it? How did the relationship progress?

**Analysis:** You want to know what type of behavior or personality is particularly challenging for the candidate to deal with, and then you need to know if the candidate has developed sufficient skills to deal with these types of people. The world of work is full of all sorts of people, and you need your employees to be able to get along with and communicate effectively with everyone. Be aware of candidates who list fairly innocuous habits as ones that disturb them.

Listen carefully to how the applicant discusses the scenario. People who truly know how to deal with challenging individuals will emphasize what was learned and how they came to appreciate interpersonal differences. People who still find it hard to deal with difficult people will talk more about the traits that made the person difficult and try to get affirmation that the person really was a creep.

107. What have you done in the past to build rapport and relationships with people?

108. Give me an example of a time when you deliberately attempted to build rapport with a coworker or customer.

109. Tell me about a time when you were able to establish rapport with a "difficult" person. How did you go about it? What were the results?

**Analysis:** Rapport-building is a specific skill that, if done effectively, can mitigate any future interpersonal difficulty. If you choose to ask this question, what you want to know is how well the candidate tries to find common ground with other people. Can the person empathize with people and understand where others are coming from? Rapport-building is very important in positions that develop and maintain long-term relationships.

110. Describe a situation where you found yourself dealing with someone who didn't like you. How did you handle it?

**Analysis:** This is a good question to ask if you sense the candidate is defensive or otherwise prone to volatile interpersonal relationships. When people answer questions about getting along with others, it is much easier to discuss situations where others are behaving in a challenging way. This question potentially uncovers areas of the applicant's personality that are challenging. Make sure to probe for details about why the other person did not like the applicant and how he or she contributed to the challenge and also facilitated a civil relationship. The biggest, and usually most transparent, red flag in this question is arrogance. Despite trying to put forth a best impression, an arrogant person will not be able to hide his disdain for someone who dared not like him.

111. Give me a specific example of a time when a coworker critized your work in front of others. How did you respond? How has that event shaped the way you communicate with others?

**Analysis:** Often the best lessons in interpersonal communication come from situations when we are at the wrong end of the communication stick. Pay attention to the details of the situation. A good follow-up probe is to ask if the candidate has ever criticized someone's work in front of other people.

112. Give me an example of a situation when you demonstrated sensitivity to diversity issues.

113. Give me an example of your ability to communicate effectively and build relationships with people regardless of cultural differences.

**Analysis:** Cultural differences are becoming more and more commonplace in the work environment. With all the other challenges to working well with other people, you certainly don't need ethnicity or cultural discrimination coming into play. The desired answer to these questions is one that minimizes cultural differences and offers a tolerant view of the world and its people. Look for the candidate to use socially appropriate terms for other cultures and to speak inclusively of other cultures rather than an "us" and "them" type of response.

114. Your department is working on an important project. During the course of the project, you recognize a potential problem with its implementation. What do you do?

115. During the course of this same project, you have an idea that has the potential to improve the project but you are in a lower-level position that may not get respect from upper management. What do you do?

**Analysis:** Assertiveness is an important consideration in interpersonal relationships. You want the candidate to be confident and willing to speak his or her mind in all situations. The ability to do this often stems from a well-developed method for dealing with opposition and even rudeness. Look for specific details that indicate the candidate is assured and confident with his or her own level of interpersonal ability.

116. One of your coworkers has a trait or habit that affects his relationships with other coworkers and customers. It is a difficult trait to mention but you feel it must be brought to his or her attention. How do you handle the situation?

**Analysis:** This question deals with a candidate's honesty and straightforwardness when dealing with other people. What you want to pay attention to is whether or not the candidate can get his or her point across sensitively and considerately, making sure to preserve the other person's dignity in the process. There are many self-proclaimed "tell-it-like-it-is" people who are upfront with others, but they come across as rude and insulting. The effective communicator approaches the situation with empathy, putting himself or herself in the other person's shoes. The ineffective communicator just wants the other person to change regardless of that person's feelings or ability to change.

117. It is often necessary to adjust our method or style of communicating to meet the needs of the individual or group we are addressing. Give me an example of a time when you used a different approach or interpersonal style to more effectively communicate with a peer or subordinate.

118. Describe a situation in which you were able to effectively "read" another person and guide your actions by your understanding of their needs and values.

119. Describe an example of a time when you had to approach several people for support or cooperation, who you considered quite different from one another. What did you have to do differently with each person? How did you know what to do differently?

120. Describe a situation in which your first attempt to sell an idea failed. How did you react to this? What other approaches did you try?

**Analysis:** The core of interpersonal skill is the ability to adjust one's responses to suit the situation and person with which one is dealing. What you ideally want to hear is an example that demonstrates the candidate can use a different style to deal with different people. If the candidate's previous examples involved using empathy and building rapport, then the answer to this question might involve the use of compassion or reason or active listening. What you want to know is whether or not the candidate has more than one or two tools in his or her interpersonal skill toolbox.

121. Some situations require us to express ideas or opinions in a very tactful and careful way. Tell me about a time when you were successful in this type of situation.

**Analysis:** Tact is so very important, and it is what constitutes the difference between honesty and rudeness. You need to know that your employees can assert themselves and communicate confidently but always with an eye to maintaining tact and professionalism. Cues for professional behavior are examples that exhibit keeping calm, mediating, compromising and placating when necessary.

122. Describe a work situation that required you to really listen and display compassion to a coworker/employee who was telling you about a personal or sensitive situation.

123. Describe a recent situation in which what was really going on with someone else was much more complicated than it might have seemed on the surface.

**Analysis:** In many workplaces, coworkers become an extended family of sorts, and despite every intention not to get too personal at work, it often cannot be avoided, particularly in supervisory or management roles when an employee needs coaching or even counseling. The key in this circumstance is to maintain a certain level of objectivity and distance. A good answer to this type of question is one that includes helping the person help himself rather than jumping in and trying to the solve the problem for him.

124. What, in your opinion, are the key ingredients for developing and maintaining successful business relationships? Give me examples of how you practice these skills.

**Analysis:** Figure out what the candidate values in terms of business goals. Ideally, you want the candidate to discuss various interpersonal skills that foster and enhance relationships, but the key to this question is the fact that it relates to business relationships, not personal ones. Probe to find out where profitability and strategy fit into the equation to make sure the candidate is not so relationship-focused that the overall needs of the business are compromised.

125. Describe a situation in which you developed an effective win/win relationship with a stakeholder or client. How did you go about building the relationship?

**Analysis:** It is important to establish whether or not the candidate appreciates the difference between compromising to solve a conflict or collaborating to get to a win/win relationship. What you don't want is an employee who compromises all over the place and calls it successful interpersonal skills. Effective interpersonal skills are those that get both parties to a place of satisfaction without either having to give up anything to get there.

126. Tell me about a time when you relied on a contact in your network to help you with a work-related task or problem.

**Analysis:** Generally, people who have well-developed interpersonal skills also are well liked and well connected. Find out if the candidate keeps in touch with contacts. This is a very good clue that the relationship is solid and based on mutual respect and admiration.

127. Give me an example of when you identified with someone else's difficulties at work. What, if anything, did you do to help them?

128. Describe a situation when you were criticized for being too concerned about the difficulties of others.

**Analysis:** Find out if the candidate equates interpersonal skills with meddling. The person who is forever concerned about everyone's welfare at work is more often the cause of conflict than the champion for change. Watch out for the candidate who emphasizes the problem his coworker was facing rather than his own actions in the situation. Solution-oriented people help the workplace develop and problem-oriented people look for things to gripe about.

129. Describe a time that politics at work affected your job. How did you handle it?

**Analysis:** It is next to impossible to avoid workplace politics, and interpersonal skills are the best way to deal with the unfortunate reality. What you want to discover in this case is where the candidate draws the line between managing within a political environment and contributing to the office politics. A person with good interpersonal skills will try to stay as neutral as possible and behave professionally at all times.

## Interview Questions for Assessing Conflict-Resolution Skills

130. In any field, conflicts will often arise between coworkers. How have you resolved a conflict with a coworker?

131. Describe a situation where you had a conflict with another individual, and how you dealt with it. What was the outcome? How did you feel about it?

132. Tell me about a situation where you were involved in a conflict. What did you do to resolve that conflict?

133. Tell me about the most memorable time when you had a personal conflict with another employee at work. How did you deal with the conflict? Why did you take this approach? How did your relationship with the person finally turn out?

134. Tell me about a difficult situation where it was desirable for you to keep a positive attitude.

**Analysis:** Conflict is inevitable and relatively frequent. The actual conflict situation that the candidate chooses to relay is an excellent source of information about what really triggers his or her personal conflicts. What you need to determine is whether or not the candidate's triggers are more or less frequent in your workplace. If the scenario involves a difference of opinion or a slight miscommunication, that person may be less attractive as an employee than one who cites a time when he or she was the victim of outright deceit or grievous behavior.

Obviously, the resolution aspect of the question is important and the candidate can be counted on to use those skills in future conflicts, but what you want to avoid is hiring someone who views minor, everyday occurrences as conflicts requiring full-fledged conflict-resolution skills.

135. Describe the way you handled a specific problem involving others with differing values, ideas and beliefs in your current/previous job.

136. Tell me about a time when you had to resolve a difference of opinion with a coworker/customer/supervisor. How do you feel you showed respect?

**Analysis:** A difference of opinion or core values is very often the basis of conflict and the type that is most difficult to resolve. The way a person sets out to work with people who are fundamentally different than himself or herself says a great deal about the person's ability to deal with differences in general. The bottom line in business is to maintain respect and professionalism at all times. These questions can yield valuable information about how the candidate deals with core personality and values differences. If he or she can provide a solid example in this category, then chances are his or her conflict-resolution skills are at least above average.

137. Give me a specific example of a time when you had to address an angry customer. What was the problem and what was the outcome? How would you assess your role in defusing the situation?

138. Describe a situation when a customer was frustrated with you because you didn't understand what he or she was saying. What did you do? What were the results?

139. Give me an example of a time when you sensed that a customer or client was upset even though they did not specifically say so. What cues did you use to make that judgment? What did you do? What were the results?

**Analysis:** Coworkers can be difficult but customers can sometimes be nasty. A customer does not have to face you the next day, or ever again, so he can be as rude as he wants, vent his anger however he wants, and be as disrespectful as he wants. Therein lies the reason that customers can frazzle even the most calm and collected employee. What you want to do is try to determine the candidate's breaking point. Where does the candidate draw the line between the customer always being right and the customer being downright wrong? Ultimately you want an employee who knows his or her limits and recognizes when the situation is best handled by someone in another position or with more authority. Probe until you are satisfied the employee went to appropriate lengths to resolve the situation without needlessly compromising the business or the relationship.

140. Tell me about a conflict you have had with a superior. How did you resolve the conflict? How did you work towards mending the relationship with that superior?

141. Tell me about the manager/supervisor/team leader who was the most difficult to work for. How did you handle this difficult relationship?

**Analysis:** Conflicts with superiors should be kept to a minimum, and if and when they do occur, they must be handled with the utmost tact and respect. Egalitarian workplaces are espoused a great deal, but when push comes to shove, someone is in charge and is responsible for employee supervision. What you, as the interviewer, want to know is how well the candidate respects lines of authority, however informal, and how he or she operates within the system. It is also vital to know how long the conflict lingered before it was dealt with and how successful the relationship was after the attempts at resolution.

142. Tell me about a time when you were assigned to a team that had a coworker you did not particularly like. How did you manage to make the team project successful while dealing with your personal feelings?

143. Give me an example of a situation where you had difficulties with a team member. What, if anything, did you do to resolve the difficulties?

**Analysis:** Interpersonal skills are all the more important when working within a team environment, so it is important to understand how the candidate deals with conflict in this particular situation. The information you are most interested in is the nature of the conflict between the team members. The resolution portion should be no different than when dealing with coworkers, in general, but what is quite revealing is the factors that led up to the conflict in the first place. Use the information given to assess whether or not the candidate is well suited to teamwork and probe to uncover his or her true feelings about teamwork.

144. Tell me about a time you had to "choose your battles carefully."

**Analysis:** Even the most interpersonally gifted individual needs to know when to leave well enough alone. Just because a person can resolve a conflict when one arises does not mean he or she should go around looking for causes to champion. Effective interpersonal skills are evident when a person realizes that differences and conflict are natural aspects of human relations and learns to operate within a slightly conflicted environment. If a person made it her mission to solve all the conflict in a workplace, she would certainly have no time to do the productive work she is paid for, so knowing when to "let it go" is a valuable asset.

145. Tell me about a time when someone has lost his or her temper at you in a business environment.

**Analysis:** A question that requires a candidate to discuss someone else's poor behavior is very revealing. The candidate is telling you what characteristics are most offensive to him or her; use that information to determine how well he or she will fit within your current work environment.

146. Tell me about a time when you saw a potential conflict between yourself and another coworker or between two of your coworkers. What did you do to help prevent the conflict?

**Analysis:** This question is designed to determine whether a candidate believes "an ounce of prevention is worth a pound of cure." Astute individuals will pick up on conflict clues before the situation escalates and can use their skills to resolve the issue before it even has a chance to materialize. What you need to determine is whether or not the prevention was warranted and helpful. Probe to find out what the outcome was and whether or not the situation has reoccurred. Don't let the candidate confuse actual resolution of a conflict with prevention. What you want to know is how the conflict was derailed before it even started.

## Application: Interpersonal/Conflict-Resolution Skills Questions

### Applicant: Charles Davenport

### Position: Administrative Assistant

Interviewer: "There are many employees in our organization and, as Administrative Assistant, you will work with many of them. Please tell me about the relationships you have with key people at your current workplace."

Interviewee: "Well, right now I work mainly with three people: my boss, the accounting clerk and the receptionist. My boss and I have a fabulous relationship—she really understands how I work and she lets me work as autonomously as possible, which is really helpful. She is also a generally positive person, so she doesn't bring the mood down if she having difficultly with something. My relationship with our receptionist is also very good—we are cross-trained on a lot of functions, so we help each other out and it's a very give-and-take relationship. The accounting clerk, on the other hand, is a little more difficult to get along with. She tends to be moody and quite focused on her own role and specific duties. Not so much a team player as I prefer to work with. Having said that, though, we do have a respectful work relationship; it is just much more business-like and curt than other relationships I have at work."

Interviewer: "Tell me more about this relationship you have with the accounting clerk. Can you describe the last time you encountered difficulty? What happened and what was the result?"

Interviewee: "It was last week actually. She was in crunch time because it was the end of our quarter, and her volume of work is much greater during key reporting periods. I knew that so I tried to do as much as I could without requesting help or information from her. However, my boss really needed some current expense figures broken down for a report she was working on and had asked me to do the round work. That was fine except I needed the overall figures and typical breakdown from Virginia, the accounting clerk. I e-mailed her first, hoping she would get to it when she had a spare moment, as it wasn't critical for me yet. When she didn't respond all day or the next morning, I went and asked her personally. I stood at her cubicle and waited until she noticed me, then I asked if she had a second. She snapped, "No, I don't have a second," and she asked me to not pester her when she was plainly concentrating on something. I apologized and left. Then at break I asked her if she had a few minutes for me in the afternoon. She exploded and said that she was on her break and did not want to bothered with work details. I decided that I wasn't going to get anywhere with her so I talked to my boss and she decided that it was okay to leave the report information until after Virginia had a chance to catch-up."

Interviewer: "Okay, can you tell me about another time you had difficulties with someone on the job other than Virginia? What was the situation and how did you handle it?"

Interviewee: "Well, this guy in marketing started asking me to do a bunch of his correspondence, and I did it for a while because I had time. Then I got quite busy and I had to say that I couldn't do things for him anymore. He got quite peeved and started acting rude and condescending to me in front of other coworkers. Eventually I had enough, and I made an appointment to talk to my boss about the situation. She hadn't even known I was doing work for him in the first place so she was very glad I brought the situation to her attention. She went and talked to the Sales Manager and the guy hasn't bothered me since. They have also since hired a part-time assistant to help with administrative tasks in that department."

This portion of the interview yielded some very interesting facts about Charles and the way he deals with people. It seems he gets along very well with people when there are no issues to deal with or when the person is a good match for his personality. However, when he encounters difficulty, he hands over the responsibility of dealing with the problem to his superior. In the first scenario it was easy to see why he might have enlisted the help of someone else to work with Virginia.

The interviewer was very wise, though, to ask about another

work conflict situation. With the second example you begin to get a fuller picture that this guy has not developed skills to deal with interpersonal conflict on his own. It also revealed some interesting information about his work priorities—he was doing unauthorized work and would have continued doing so until, presumably, his boss found out.

*Probe, probe, and probe some more—you never know what gems of information you will pick up.*

*Empathy is described as the ability to identify with and care about others.*

# 5

# Empathy and Service Orientation

Empathy is described as the ability to identify with and care about others. Customer service is the ability to serve customers in a manner that builds loyalty and repeat business. These two competencies are closely related, as one must have a well-developed sense of empathy in order to deal effectively and humanely with customers.

What you, as the interviewer, need to be concerned about is whether or not the person in front of you treats people with care and compassion without any expectation of rewards or benefit for himself or herself. In the workplace, employees deal with a variety of customers, or stakeholders, and each one must be dealt with in a manner that promotes respect and builds the relationship in preparation for future interaction.

The qualities that you are looking for include:

- Recognition that all people are different.

- Acceptance of those differences.

- Ability to see situations through different perspectives.

- Acknowledgement that treating people with dignity is an expectation of the job and does not require personal gain in return.

- Understanding that great customer service is an expectation of the job and does not require personal gain in return.

While all workplaces will have different views on customer service and the exact administration of service, the common elements of empathy, respect and dignity are necessarily present in a sustainable work environment.

## Interview Questions for Assessing Empathy

147. Give me an example of when you identified with someone else's difficulties at work. What, if anything, did you do to help them?

**Analysis:** With a question like this, you are looking for answers that display genuine concern for the other individual. People with natural empathy will focus on what the other person was going through and will be able to pull you into the scenario, whereas people who are "faking it" will be less convincing and compelling. Trust your instincts with a question like this, and ask a lot of follow-up probes to make sure that the scenario being explained is real.

It is also important to evaluate the difficulty that is being described. Be wary of an example that deals with a fellow employee's personal life; better answers are ones that highlight how the candidate helped a coworker with a job-related task or issue.

148. Give me an example of a time when a company policy or action hurt people. What, if anything, did you do to mitigate the negative consequences to people?

**Analysis:** What you will be looking for is a candidate who clearly understands and recognizes the appropriate boundaries within organizations. While it is important to empathize with the plights of others, it is equally important to know when something is within your control or beyond it. Empathy is an important characteristic to demonstrate at all levels of a company and with all coworkers, peers and subordinates.

149. Describe a situation when you were criticized for being too concerned about the difficulties of others.

**Analysis:** Here, again, you are looking for a balance between wanting to help someone and making sure that the effort to do so is not wasted, inappropriate or counterproductive. Empathy is certainly important, but it cannot be allowed to overshadow one's day-to-day activities, duties or responsibilities. The effective application of empathy is such that it enhances the workplace, rather than deters from it.

150. Give me an example of when you went out of your way to help someone. What were your thoughts and feelings about that situation?

**Analysis:** The candidate with a solid grasp of the notion of empathy will express thoughts and feelings such as self-satisfaction, accomplishment and enhanced self-esteem. People who generally embrace empathy do it for their own pleasure, rather than what they hope to gain from the situation. What you're looking for, as an interviewer, is a candidate whose answer emphasizes how good he or she felt about the experience, and who can demonstrate that his or her actions were well-received.

151. Give me an example of when you had to make a decision where the choices were either in favor of your

own self-interest or someone else's. What were your thoughts and feelings? What did you do?

**Analysis:** This is a very difficult question for candidates to answer. There is no clear right or wrong answer, and it is confusing as well as stressful. Your job will be to evaluate the response in relation to the culture within your own organization, the expectations placed on the position for which the person is applying, and your own sense of the honesty of the answer. What will be important in the answer is a well-thought-out and clearly articulated means for evaluating the two choices and a solid argument for why one choice was chosen over the other.

152. What positive contributions have you made to your community or society?

153. Give me an example of when you were given special recognition or acknowledgement for your contributions to the disadvantaged.

**Analysis:** Depending on the culture or overall purpose of your organization, this may be an important factor when considering employment. Every company places a different value on community service, community involvement and other unselfish activities.

154. Can you recall a time when a person's cultural background affected your approach to a work situation?

**Analysis:** Cultural differences are often at the root of many interpersonal conflicts at work. Regardless of the position for which you're hiring, the successful candidate must be able to demonstrate that he or she has a tolerance for differences in culture, as well as opinion. Listen carefully to the scenario being described. Be wary of answers that seem generalized or trivial. Very few people these days have not encountered a situation in which cultural differences played a significant role. Empathy is not something that can be faked or embellished—look for genuine concern and honesty. The more detailed the response and emotional the reaction, the higher the likelihood of the scenario being real.

155. Can you recall a time when you gave feedback to a coworker who was not tolerant of others?

**Analysis:** People who display empathy in all aspects of their lives are sensitive to situations, where others are not acting particularly empathic. What is important in this answer is whether or not the person dealt with the coworker in a manner that would, in itself, be considered empathic. Remember, a person who is skilled in empathy will deal with all people and all situations with the utmost respect, dignity and compassion.

## Interview Questions for Assessing Service Orientation

156. Describe the steps you would take if a customer came to you with a problem you could solve at your job level.

157. Tell me about a time when you did your best to resolve a customer or client concern and the individual still was not satisfied. What did you do next?

**Analysis:** Customer complaints or concerns are perhaps the most difficult situations in which to display empathy, self-control and a commitment to service. However, these are the exact traits that are required for any position that deals with the general public or internal clients and customers. What you're looking for in the candidate's response to this question is the level of commitment he or she demonstrated while trying to resolve the customer's needs. Actually solving the problem is not as important in this answer as the steps the candidate took along the way. Evaluate the answer based on thoroughness and a commitment to understanding the client's concerns and then taking the appropriate action.

158. Tell me about a time when you exceeded a customer's expectations. How did it make the customer feel? How did it make you feel?

159. Describe a situation where you were given exceptional customer service. What made it stand out?

160. Give me an example of when you were given special recognition or acknowledgement for going the extra mile to satisfy a customer.

**Analysis:** In order for a person to give excellent service, he or she needs to recognize what outstanding service truly entails. The best way to do this is to think empathically about one's own experiences with customer service. What you're looking for is a candidate who places value on helping a customer to feel satisfied, dignified, respected, understood, and appreciated. Look for these types of emotional cues with the candidate's answer to determine whether or not the person has a solid understanding of the foundations of customer-service excellence.

161. Tell me about a time that you had to go out of your immediate network/job duties to help a customer.

162. Describe the steps you would take if a customer came to you with a problem that was beyond your knowledge and/or responsibilities.

163. Describe a recent situation when you didn't know with whom you needed to speak in organization to get something done. What did you do?

164. Tell me about a time when you didn't have the answer to a question that a customer wanted right away. What did you do? What was the final outcome?

**Analysis:** Providing excellent customer service requires doing more than simply what you can do. Look for answers where the candidate recognizes his or her own limitations in terms of authority, responsibility or experience and how willing the candidate is to seek outside help. If an employee applies empathy to a customer-service situation, then he or she will be willing to do whatever it takes to satisfy the customer or at least make sure every option has been explored.

Another aspect to good service orientation is a thorough understanding of the resources available in order to satisfy a client. Make sure to evaluate the candidate based on desire to help as well as efficient and effective methods of attaining the help required.

165. Tell me about the worst customer you ever had and how you dealt with him or her.

166. Describe the steps you would use to calm an angry customer.

**Analysis:** Some candidates may be reluctant to answer a question like this one, claiming that none of their clients were the worst or angry because they have always been successful at turning any situation into a positive one. If this happens, rephrase the question, making it clear that you're truly interested in hearing about one of the most difficult customers the candidate has ever had to deal with. Continue to probe until you get a specific answer.

What you're looking for in the answer is the specific triggers that the candidate may have in terms of behaviors he or she finds difficult to deal with. The less typical or common behavioral trigger, the lower the likelihood that the candidate will become flustered, stressed or agitated by consumers in general. You should also make sure that the qualities or behaviors mentioned are problematic for the average person. What you don't want in your workplace is an employee whose triggers include behaviors that are not expected to cause any difficulty.

The second aspect of this question is the actual steps the candidate took in order to resolve the situation. Look for answers that indicate the interviewee handled the situation on his or her own and only solicited outside help that was absolutely necessary. Evaluate the answer based on your own sense of how effective and appropriate the intervention was. Look for signs that the candidate's natural style of resolving customer difficulties is in line with the style espoused by your organization.

167. Tell me about a time that a customer came to you angry (not necessarily at you) and how you worked with that customer to solve the issue.

168. Have you ever had a customer get angry at something that wasn't your fault? If so, please explain.

**Analysis:** Often when you work with customers, you are thrust into a situation where you need to deal with a problem that simply was not your fault. A natural tendency in situations like this is to abdicate your responsibility and refer the customer to the person who created the problem in the first place. Not only is this response unacceptable, it also displays a lack of empathy. The customer only wants his or her issue resolved; you need employees who understand this and are willing to take responsibility and help the customer become satisfied.

Look for answers that demonstrate the candidate took immediate action, took responsibility for the problem, and gathered whatever resources were necessary to resolve the situation.

169. Why is follow-up important in customer service?

170. A customer comes in with a small request. The small request is not a priority for you but you realize that

they have the potential to use your services extensively in the future. How do you ensure that the customer has a good experience and will want to come back to you in the future?

171. Describe a situation when you took a stand for a customer.

**Analysis:** What you looking for in answers to this question is the actual level of commitment the candidate has to providing excellent customer service. The employee never knows if a customer was satisfied or otherwise pleased with the service received unless he or she does something to verify that satisfaction.

The answer doesn't need to be an elaborate scheme, where the customer is phoned or contacted a few days or weeks after the incident. It can simply be escorting the customer to the door, engaging in pleasant small talk, acknowledging the customer the next time he or she comes in, or anything else that actively promotes a positive end to the situation.

172. Give us an example of a time when you used your customer service philosophy to deal with a perplexing problem.

**Analysis:** This is a question that involves organizational fit. You want to know what the candidate's customer-service philosophy is, and whether or not that philosophy will work in your organization. A candidate's philosophy will be based on his or her values and principles, and it is important that your employees have similar methods for dealing with adversity and can embrace the company's philosophy without compromising their own ideals.

## Application: Empathy/Service-Orientation Skills Questions
**Applicant: Charles Davenport**

**Position: Administrative Assistant**

Interviewer: "In this role in administration you will be surrounded by a variety of people. Can you tell me about a time when you needed to understand another person's cultural background in order to work effectively with him or her?"

Interviewee: "Actually, at my current workplace we have a transfer student from Australia working with us for the summer. She is doing a lot of odd jobs and trying to learn about what it is like working in an American office. As a result, she does a lot of little projects for me, and at first her work ethic really bothered me. She was too relaxed and too methodical for me, and I found myself getting irritated. She was doing the jobs fine, she just wasn't doing them with the same zest that I would have, and I knew it was my issue, not hers. Since I'd never been to Australia or knew any Australians, I invited her over for dinner with our family and we got to talking about her culture and what life was like "down under." Turns out she was equally perplexed by our American vigor—things in Australia move at a slower pace and there is not that sense of urgency we experience here. I felt so good after talking with her, and now I understand where she is coming from."

Interviewer: "As an Administrative Assistant you will often be asked to do things by a variety of internal clients. I'm interested in understanding your approach when dealing with people who may not be satisfied with your responsiveness."

Interviewee: "Hmmm, I must say that I am very responsive to people's requests. I think it is important to keep everyone satisfied, and as long as my boss is okay with the work I'm doing for other people, then I'm okay with it."

Interviewer: "Okay, but what I'm really interested in

hearing is a specific incident where someone made a request of you that maybe you didn't have time for or couldn't get to. How did the negative feedback make you feel and what did you do?"

Interviewee:     "There was this time when the sales department was getting me to run their monthly statistics. I really didn't like doing it and didn't think it was really my responsibility so I went to the sales manager and asked for a meeting with him as well as my boss. I knew I couldn't resolve the issue on my own and I knew he needed the stats run, so I was hoping we could all figure out a solution. Turns out the sales manager was considering hiring some part-time help and my boss agreed that I was too busy to be doing the work, so everything ended up fine. The sales manger appreciated my honesty and I felt good knowing that I just didn't dig in my heels but tried to work out a solution."

The interviewer did a good job of explaining the basis for asking the question. Often that explanation at the beginning of the question helps the candidate choose a relevant example and it also puts him or her at ease knowing you have a real reason for asking the question other than simply trying to trip him or her up.

103

Notice how Charles tried to avoid the "negatively" slanted internal customer question. This is a common avoidance technique, and the candidate will usually slip into a soap-box type answer that everyone is expected to agree with. The interviewer rephrased the question and probed for more information and it worked.

As we get to know more and more about Charles, it is becoming clearer what makes him tick and what his general outlook on life is. Turns out he is quite empathic. This is a bit surprising given his less than stellar interpersonal skills, but what it does indicate is that he has the foundation for resolving conflict and perhaps he just needs some specific training and more experience dealing with actual conflict.

*Be on the lookout for areas where the candidate may simply require professional development in order to become fully competent in an area.*

# 6
# Problem Solving

The ability to solve problems is a skill that oftentimes goes unrecognized. People who are good at solving problems often do so at an almost subconscious level. Your role in the interview is to draw out the automatic process that a candidate goes through when solving a problem and then evaluate the overall effectiveness of the approach.

Elements to look for when identifying good problem solvers include:

- Uses a systematic approach.

- Avoids jumping to conclusions.

- Gathers data and facts.

- Deals quickly with the immediate effects of the problem.

- Identifies the most likely cause and contributors to the problem.

- Recognizes that not all problems involve complex solutions.

- Looks at a problem from a practical standpoint first.

- Identifies alternative ways to deal with the problem.

- Uses resources (human and otherwise) to improve the process.

- Thinks proactively to avoid problems that have not yet been identified.

## Interview Questions for Assessing Problem-Solving Skills

173. Describe a specific problem you solved for your employer. How did you approach the problem? What role did others play? What was the outcome?

174. Describe a difficult problem that you tried to solve. How did you identify the problem? How did you go about trying to solve it?

175. Describe a complicated problem you had to deal with. How did you identify it or gain a better understanding of it?

176. Describe a major problem you have faced and how you dealt with it.

177. Describe a work-related problem you had to face recently? What procedures did you use to deal with it? What was the outcome?

178. Think about a complex project or assignment that you have been assigned. What approach did you take to complete it?

179. Describe a time when you had to analyze a problem and generate a solution.

180. Tell me about a situation where you had to solve a problem or make a decision that required careful thought. What did you do?

**Analysis:** What you are looking for is an answer that demonstrates the candidate applies a systematic problem-solving method. What you want to make sure of is that this person will not jump headfirst into the problem without taking the steps necessary to make sure that the actions are not going to exacerbate or in any way contribute to the problem. Problem solving is stressful, and sometimes the immediate reaction is to go into "fix it" mode. Unfortunately, a problem can't be fixed unless the causes and contributing factors have been identified.

Look for candidates who recognize that problem solving has two separate focuses: short-term and long-term. The short-term focus is on doing what needs to be done to get things up and running until the entire situation is dealt with. The long-term focus is on solving the problem and making sure it does not happen again.

You want indications that a potential employee is able to remain focused and concentrate on the task at hand and not get to caught up in either the short- or long-term end. The balance between the two is critical, and those people who can manage that balance will be invaluable in a problem-solving role.

181. Describe for me a major project that you worked on where things did not go exactly as planned.

182. Describe a time when you failed to solve a problem.

**Analysis:** When you ask a question about a negative event, you want to make sure that the answer is not trivial or deceptive. Candidates don't like talking about their failures, but we all know that everyone has had disappointment, and what you want to know is how the candidate handled the adverse situation. What did he or she learn from the experience? Probe to find out whether a similar situation occurred after the experience and how the candidate's reaction was different. Did he or she apply what was learned from the first experience and how successful was the second attempt? The focus here is not so much on what they did wrong, but how they internalized that information and used it, hopefully, to improve their performance in the future.

183. Think of a time when you encountered a problem achieving a goal or objective. Tell me about the process you used to solve the problem.

**Analysis:** Here, again, what you are looking for is the details to systematic explanation of the process the candidate uses when faced with a problem. Evaluate the approach based on your experiences within the organization and how well you think the approach will fit within the context. Be sure to look for clues to indicate frustration and/or stress levels that might be counterproductive to the problem-solving process. Encourage the candidate to talk about the emotional aspects of problem solving, and determine how well the person handles diversity in general.

184. Tell me about a time when you had to identify the underlying causes of a problem.

**Analysis:** People often mistake quick fixes with good problem solving; your job is to determine what level of sophisticated problem solving the candidate possesses. Ask the candidate what it was about the situation that made him or her want or need to figure out the underlying causes and how successful the end result was because of it.

185. Tell me about a problem that needed a fast response and how you handled it.

186. Describe an instance when you had to think on your feet to extricate yourself from a difficult situation.

**Analysis:** This question explores when and where the candidate uses good judgment in determining how quick of a response to a problem is needed. It's important for employees to know that the root causes of a problem need to be explored and rectified, however. There are times that call for quick action. Evaluate the example the candidate talks about to determine whether or not quick action was truly the best option. Other things to consider include the appropriateness of the action, the practicality of the solution, the reaction of other stakeholders, and the overall result. Because this is a problem-solving question, make sure to determine if further investigation was carried out or initiated by the candidate.

187. Tell me about a time when you recognized a problem or an opportunity before anyone else. What happened? Have you ever recognized a problem before your boss or others in the organization? Explain.

188. Describe a time when you anticipated potential problems and developed preventative measures.

189. Describe a situation in which you forecasted a problem and prepared a strategy for handling it.

**Analysis:** These types of questions highlight an important aspect of problem solving: proactivity. Solving a problem after the fact is good, but averting a problem altogether is better. What you are looking for in the candidate's response is the type of clues the person looks for when identifying potential problem areas. Make sure the problem or opportunity discussed warrants the time and energy expended in the effort to avoid or prepare for it. What you don't want is an employee who looks for problems that may or may not be there and takes time away from more productive work. Make sure to ask for details of the outcome and whether or not the solution or opportunity was adequately addressed.

190. Tell me about a time when you missed an obvious solution to a problem.

**Analysis:** What you are assessing in this question is the level of understanding the candidate has with regard to gathering facts and information before trying to solve a problem. It is very important that employees force themselves to understand the whole situation and think the options through before acting to solve the entire problem. What you are looking for is recognition from the candidate that he or she did not consider all possibilities or use judgment or logic to solve the problem, but rather relied more on instinct and gut feelings.

These things are tough for an interviewee to admit, so you are looking for candor and honesty as well as compelling evidence that the person learned from the situation. The best way to figure that out is to ask how they have performed in similar situations and how well they applied their new knowledge.

191. Tell me about a situation where when you were first presented a problem, you had absolutely no idea how to approach it and how you eventually solved the problem.

192. Tell me about a time when your manager was unavailable and you had to solve an immediate problem. What did you do and what was the outcome?

193. Describe a situation in which you effectively developed a solution to a problem by combining different perspectives or approaches.

**Analysis:** Here you are looking for a candidate's ability to be creative and innovative in problem solving. Sure, they can have a tried-and-true method all worked out, but often life throws a wrench into the best-laid plans. What you are trying to assess is how well the person can adapt quickly and apply the same principles of systematic processes, logic and judgment to new and unfamiliar situations.

Be especially curious about the resources the person used to begin the problem-solving process. Who did they contact for help or advice and how useful was the information received? A very common element in solving problems is knowing who to turn to when you hit a road block. As always, make sure the end result was effective, and evaluate the candidate on his or her ability to perform a difficult task under trying circumstances.

194. Describe a recent situation in which you asked for advice.

195. Describe a recent situation in which you asked for help.

**Analysis:** The key to problem solving is recognizing when you have a problem and need help. What you, as the interviewer, want to know is how open the candidate is to actually asking for assistance. It is important to know how to solve problems, but high-performing individuals are the ones most willing to ask for assistance or advice because they know doing so does not indicate weakness or ignorance; it simply acknowledges that they know they don't know everything.

In the same vein, make sure the example described is not one where the candidate was reasonably expected to perform the task on his or her own. If you are in doubt, make sure you probe for all the details and make sure to evaluate the candidate's tendency to ask for help with the overall expectations within your organization.

196. Describe a challenge or opportunity you identified based on your industry knowledge and how you developed a strategy to respond to it.

197. Describe a time when you used your business knowledge to understand a specific business situation.

**Analysis:** Often specific business issues require specialized approaches. If you decide to ask this question it may because the job for which the candidate is applying requires a set, problem-solving approach. In other cases, you might be interested in finding out how the candidate incorporates technical or otherwise specific information in his or her problem-solving approach. When evaluating the answer, look for evidence that the person used his or her specialized skills to add value to the problem-solving process rather than further complicating the issue by adding irrelevant information.

Follow up with questions about the process and outcome to ensure that the example used was successful because of the candidate's involvement and expertise.

## Application: Problem-Solving Skills Questions
### Applicant: Charles Davenport

### Position: Administrative Assistant

Interviewer: "As an Administrative Assistant you will encounter many problems and setbacks: some minor and some quite significant. Can you describe for me the last problem you solved at work?"

Interviewee: "Yes, one of our employees was going on vacation the next week and we had recently changed our policy allowing employees to request their vacation pay before they went on vacation rather than waiting for the next scheduled payday. I know he filled out the request form because I personally received it and then forwarded it to my boss to confirm the employee had enough vacation hours to cover the request. I then returned the request form to the employee's boss for his final approval, and then he was to submit a check requisition to payroll and accounting. When the check didn't arrive, the employee came to me asking for it. I didn't know exactly what happened to the check but I did know he followed the correct process, and somewhere along the line the ball was dropped. I knew I had to get him his check. I called his boss and asked him if he had filled out the requisition. The boss had actually thought our department would fill out the requisition so the paperwork was still in his bin—untouched. I went immediately and got the boss to sign the requisition, and then took it personally to payroll and accounting and asked for a check. The employee had his check the next day and went on his vacation with no problem."

Interviewer: "Was that the end of your involvement?"

Interviewee: "No, after I had dealt with the immediate problem, I got to thinking that if this type of mix-up happened once, it was sure to happen again, and the whole reason why we changed the policy was to make things easier for the employees, not more complicated and stressful, so I asked for a meeting with my boss and explained what had happened in detail. She knew the basics from my intervention the day before, but now we talked about it in depth. I suggested we re-examine our reasons for sending the request form back to the department manager for signature, and we eventually decided to take out that step and just streamline the process so that we receive the signed request, verify the hours, if the hours are sufficient, then we send the requisition in with a carbon copy to the department manager. The fewer steps in the process, the less chance for mistakes, and we haven't had a repeat problem since."

Interviewer: "Tell me why you decided to intervene on the employee's behalf instead of concentrating on fixing the procedural problem."

Interviewee: "Well, the way I looked at it was, to fix the process may take a while—you have to analyze what went wrong and then put a plan in place to address it. This employee couldn't wait that long—he was going on vacation the next week. I guess I looked at the benefits versus the costs of helping the employee immediately and then dealing with the problem later, and it seemed the logical thing to do to make the situation right and then fix the whole thing when other people had a chance to get involved."

This time the interviewer started with a very broad question and then honed it down to get the answers he wanted. This is often a good technique because the interviewee does not know the direction the interviewer is going to go. This gives the interviewer a better chance of hearing a description that is less tailored to the situation and may reveal some potentially useful information: good or bad. Charles did a good job with the questions, and with each further prompt, he revealed important details about his problem-solving ability and the way he prioritizes issues during less than optimum conditions.

Notice that the prompts do not provide any clues for the candidate to judge whether his or her answer was good, bad or indifferent. This is an important characteristic of effective probes. Remember, you don't want to lead the candidate to an answer and you don't want the candidate to know whether or not you agree or disagree with the answer provided.

In order to get the most honest and forthright answers, you must give away very little in terms of your personal evaluation. Candidates will pick up on what you tend to approve or disapprove and censor (or augment) future answers accordingly. This doesn't mean you need to be stiff and unfriendly, just eliminate references to how you feel about certain answers, examples or responses.

*Convey neutrality and provide very few feedback cues to the interviewee.*

*Whether reaching conclusions, solving problems or making valid decisions, a productive employee needs strong analytical skills.*

# 7

# Analytical Ability

The purpose of questions regarding a person's analytical ability is to uncover how well the candidate can gather information and extract relevant data. Today's workplaces are rife with information overload, so it is imperative that employees be able to make sense of and analyze vast amounts of information efficiently and accurately. Whether reaching conclusions, solving problems or making valid decisions, a productive employee needs strong analytical skills.

Your job is to determine whether the candidate sitting before you is a sharp thinker. Does he or she recognize the need for systematic analysis and how well does he or she apply it? What you're looking for in the responses are the details of the person's approach to analyzing information. Techniques to listen for include:

- Regularly consulting other sources of information such as the Internet or publications.

- Using visual aids to facilitate the analysis process, such as flowcharts, mind maps or diagrams.

- Conducting "what if" analyses to evaluate a variety of options and outcomes.

- Using established methods to analyze information or data as prescribed by the industry or company.

- Routinely verifying conclusions and the data they are based upon for reliability and validity.

Depending on the work environment, you may be interested in a candidate's analytical skills in individual work and teamwork. Tailor your questions accordingly, and be aware that people may use different strategies depending on the situation, so it is important to get more than one example.

## Interview Questions for Assessing Analytical Skills

198. What kind of information have you been required to analyze?

**Analysis:** This is a straightforward question but it gives you the information you need to determine if the candidate's experience with analytical thinking is suitable for the position.

Some people have experience analyzing numerical data but aren't comfortable with more theoretical and abstract analysis and vice versa; you need to decide if the person's exposure to analytical material is appropriate and sufficient.

199. Describe the project or situation that best demonstrates your analytical abilities. What was your role?

200. What steps do you follow to study a problem before making a decision? Why?

201. Describe a complicated problem you have had to deal with on the job. How did you identify or gain a better understanding of that problem?

**Analysis:** What you are looking for in this answer is the candidate's overall familiarity and experience analyzing information. The more experience a person has with analysis, the more likely they will employ a lot of techniques to make sure the work is thorough. Probe to get details on the exact methods used and how the analysis contributed to a positive result.

202. Describe a situation where you have gathered and analyzed facts to arrive at a decision.

203. Tell me about a time when you used your fact-finding skills to solve a problem.

**Analysis:** The less glamorous side of analysis is the actual fact-finding. Candidates may skim over this part of the process and focus more attention on what the findings meant and how they were used. By asking a specific question about gathering facts, you will be able to evaluate the thoroughness of the applicant's approach. You should also listen for enthusiasm and a willingness to participate in all stages of analysis.

204. Can you tell me about a time when you presented complex information to a group of people? What techniques did you use in your presentation?

**Analysis:** Here is a question where you can determine the candidate's comfort level with using and then presenting visual representations for analyzing information. The saying "a picture is worth a thousand words" definitely applies to analysis, and a candidate who can create visual images to explain analytical data is very competent with the entire process. Use this question to evaluate the level of expertise the candidate has, and compare that with the level needed for the position.

205. Describe for me a time when you used a "what if" analysis of a situation. What was the issue and the outcome?

**Analysis:** The ability to use "what if" analysis is key to successful analysis of many, if not all, situations. The "what if" process does not even have to be explicit or overly formal. The answers will range from a fleeting thought of, "What if this happens?" to a fully detailed and documented analysis. Regardless of the extent of the analysis, what you need to evaluate is the candidate's recognition that "what if" analysis is critical and whether the magnitude of the analysis was appropriate given the situation.

Some people are very analytical and will analyze a situation to death whether it needs it or not. Others will just breeze through the analysis to get to the decision making. Your job is to determine whether the candidate appreciates the value in "what if" analysis and to make sure that they don't engage in elaborate analytical exercises that are not necessary.

Probe for information about the results and how well-received the analysis was. You want to be able to get a good idea of whether or not other stakeholders saw the value in the analysis.

206. Tell me about a time when you had to analyze or interpret numerical or scientific information.

207. When have you been required to analyze detailed, numeric data while being under pressure or otherwise rushed?

**Analysis:** Analyzing numbers is difficult at the best of times and requires a unique set of skills that are not required for non-numeric data. Numbers are concrete, and there is usually a right and wrong. What you want to know is how well a candidate deals with the precision required. Particularly telling is a situation where the person was under external pressure to complete the analysis. Probe to find out if corners were cut or some other sacrifice was made in order to make the deadline. Try to get the candidate to talk about the process he or she uses and what methods are used to verify accuracy and correctness.

Your job is to determine if the process is reliable. Ask for information regarding the number and type of revisions or corrections required. Does this figure change with work that is done under pressure, or does the candidate's skill and technique hold up under even the most difficult circumstances? What you need to determine is whether the candidate performs with this type of information and whether his or her experience is a good fit for the position.

208. Tell me about a time when you had to review detailed reports or documents to identify a problem.

**Analysis:** Analyzing written information is another specific skill set that requires excellent reading comprehension and the ability to identify and answer missing elements. Ask what the analysis was for and how the candidate structured the analysis.

Often when analyzing written information, the volume of documents is staggering. What you want to know is how the person organizes the analysis. One approach would be to read through everything word for word, but that is highly time-consuming and costly. What you want to know is how adept the person is at extracting relevant information and then using that information to make a thorough analysis of the problem or situation.

209. Tell me about a time when you had to analyze information and make a decision or recommendation.

**Analysis:** This is a general question designed to get the candidates talking about an analysis they were responsible for from start to finish. You want to get a complete answer that details the analytical process, and then take that to the next level by determining how confident the person is with the analysis he or she made. Eventually the analysis has to end and a decision or recommendation needs to be made. What you need to evaluate is the candidate's ability to recognize when sufficient analysis has been done and then how willing he or she is to rely on that analysis.

The second part of the question is determining how well the recommendation was received and information about the final outcome. Make sure you get the full scenario before evaluating the candidate. You will probably have to probe to get a full and complete answer. And be prepared for a question like this one to take a long time to answer. Examples of probes to use are: To whom did you make the recommendation? What was your reasoning? What kind of thought process did you go through? Why? Was the recommendation accepted? If not, why?

210. When have you found it useful to use detailed checklists/procedures to reduce potential for error on the job? Be specific.

211. What steps do you follow to study a problem in order to fully understand the situation?

**Analysis:** Here, again, are technical questions designed to uncover the specific methodology used in analysis. Checking the accuracy and reliability of data is of paramount importance because many very critical decisions hinge on the outcome of a business analysis. You need to be confident that the candidate you choose recognizes the importance of this step and is not willing to compromise accuracy for speed.

212. Describe one of your most difficult analyses.

213. Recall a time when you were assigned what you considered to be a complex project. Specifically, what steps did you take to prepare for and finish the project?

Were you happy with the outcome? What one step would you have done differently if given the chance?

214. What was the most complex assignment you have had? What was your role?

215. Please describe a situation where you had to compile a large amount of information in order to complete a task or a project.

**Analysis:** These questions are designed to get the candidate to reveal which aspects of analysis he or she is least confident with or experienced at. The situation a person feels is most complex or difficult is likely the one that brought up the most anxiety and feelings of doubt. What you are interested in is the outcome and how the situation contributed to the candidate's overall analytical ability to date.

Look for smart analysis of the person's own performance in the situation. If a person intuitively evaluates his or her own performance, that is a pretty strong indicator that analytical thinking is second nature and will be applied to all situations encountered at work and otherwise.

216. Have you ever had to review proposals submitted by a

vendor or by another team? Tell me about one of those situations.

**Analysis:** Evaluating and analyzing coworkers' and peers' work is difficult. What you want to know is how the candidate prepares for the potential hard feelings or awkwardness once the analysis is complete. This type of question involves empathy and the ability to analyze data within the entire context of a situation and not see just the facts. Remembering that people's ideas and work are attached to those facts is important, and the candidate should be able to demonstrate a sensitivity to and understanding of the interpersonal dynamics at work in a situation like this. Evaluate the appropriateness of the analytical approach as well as how the results and/or recommendations were communicated.

## Application: Analytical Skills Questions
### Applicant: Charles Davenport

### Position: Administrative Assistant

| | |
|---|---|
| Interviewer: | "I'm wondering how much experience you have had with data analysis. Can you tell me about the last analytical task you performed?" |
| Interviewee: | "Analytical? You mean solving a problem, like the last questions?" |

Interviewer:      "Not exactly. Analysis of information deals with
                  gathering together a bunch of information and
                  extracting the relevant data to make a decision,
                  come to a conclusion, or solve a problem. I'm
                  looking for more information on times when
                  you had to wade through large amounts of data
                  and compare the information or make some
                  kind of judgment about the information you
                  collected."

Interviewee:      "Oh, alright. That's easy. Just recently our
                  photocopy lease was up for renewal and my
                  boss needed to decide whether to continue
                  with the current service or try out someone
                  else. She asked me to gather information on
                  different providers in the area and what they
                  offered, their prices, that sort of thing. So I got
                  her the information, and she ended up
                  deciding to stick with our current guy."

Interviewer:      "I'd like a bit more detail. What information did
                  you provide and how did it make her decision-
                  making process easier? Walk me through what
                  you did."

Interviewee:      "I started with the Yellow Pages and made a list
                  of all the services available in our area. I called

the first company on the list and asked a bunch of questions and did the same thing with the next three or four companies. What I was finding was that I was getting slightly different information from each place, like some offered five-year leases and others three years, some included unlimited service calls; stuff like that. So because of these differences, their prices varied. What I ended up doing was making a master list of questions and then I created a spreadsheet where I was able to convert all prices to a per-year basis and then used the number of service calls we received over the last year as an average to figure out how much that would cost on a yearly basis. Eventually I came up with a pretty accurate yearly cost of the service for all of the companies. I also included a column on reputation and years in business so it wasn't all just based on dollars. I explained my reasoning to my boss and she agreed with my process and then made a decision."

Interviewer:    "From what you learned during this process, what do you think is the most important aspect when doing an analysis?"

Interviewee:    "Making sure you are comparing apples to

apples. Gathering the information was just the first part; the critical aspect was breaking down that information and making it useable."

Interviewer: "Now that you understand what I'm talking about when I refer to an analysis, what would you say is your overall experience level with analytical tasks?"

Interviewee: "Overall, I figure I've had moderate experience with it. This photocopy assignment was probably the largest analysis I've done, but I do break down training information and office costs, that sort of thing, for my boss pretty regularly. The big formal analysis is less frequent. I like it, though, and I think I have a good grasp on what it takes. My first big assignment turned out pretty good and I didn't get a lot of outside assistance so I feel confident in my ability to do analytical work, if that counts for anything."

With this scenario, the interviewer needed to explain a term in order to help Charles fully understand what was being asked of him. In this case, Charles gave an explicit clue that he wasn't clear on what analysis meant, but often you will have to pick up on an applicant's misunderstanding and quickly correct him or her. Don't feel awkward doing this; just explain that you're not getting the information you need, and place the responsibility for the misunderstanding on yourself. Never make the candidate feel ignorant or otherwise insulted; remember, it is your responsibility to extract the information you need to make a solid hiring decision.

After one prompt for more detail, Charles provided a very detailed account of the steps he took in his analysis. What the interviewer did next was ask opinion questions to get a sense of how Charles felt about his performance. The example was very clear and included a very well-thought-out and executed analysis. The interviewer didn't feel the need for more detailed explanations so he chose to get information on Charles' experience with analysis in a different way.

Opinion questions are just that—someone's opinion, which means they are neither right nor wrong, they simply are. However, in this case, the opinion questions gave the interviewer valuable information about analytical skills without getting into another detailed description of an analysis. You may want to use this technique for competencies that you are interested in but don't necessarily have time to cover completely. If you do choose to use opinion questions (or other non-behavioral questions), make sure you include them in your structured interview plan and ask them of all the candidates.

*Consider including opinion and other non-behavioral questions in your structured interview.*

# 8
# Decision Making

The ability to make good decisions is a finely tuned skill that requires good judgment and self-confidence. Good judgment is the ability to know how to balance making decisions based on facts, data and observations versus using intuition and gut feelings. The more times a person makes a successful decision, the more confident he or she becomes in making decisions, and subsequent decisions are then made with more conviction. What you, as the interviewer, need to determine is where on the decision-making cycle the candidate is.

The questions to ask in the decision-making section should focus on the candidate's awareness of his or her own decision-making process. How much objectivity versus subjectivity goes into the decision, and was there a difference in emphasis when the decision turned out to be poor or excellent? Three components you are looking for are:

## Judgment

Demonstration of a balance between reliance on facts and intuition.

## Self-confidence

Demonstration of a belief in one's own capability to make a good decision.

## Persistence

Demonstration of perseverance and stamina in the face of negative feedback or other adversity.

When evaluating candidates in this section, be on the lookout for confidence in the areas of judgment, analysis and instincts.

Equally important is the ability to make decisions under pressure or time constraints. The workplace is often fast-paced, and candidates who need to uncover every detail before taking action will hold back progress. Look for an appropriate balance between acting too hastily and not acting at all. Finally, you need to understand how the candidate will react in a situation where the decision is criticized or even turns out to be wrong. There is always an element of uncertainty in any decision, so choosing a candidate who can handle constructive feedback and take responsibility are crucial in the workplace.

## Interview Questions for Assessing Decision-Making Skills

217. Tell me about a difficult decision you had to make. What information led you to make the decision that you made? What other possible solutions were there? What was the final outcome?

218. What was the biggest decision you made in the past three months? Tell me about the process you went through to make it.

219. What was the most difficult decision you made in the last six months? What made it difficult? How did you formulate this decision?

220. Give me an example of a time you had to make a difficult decision.

221. Give me a specific example of a time when you used good judgment and logic to make a decision.

222. What is the most difficult decision you've had to make? How did you arrive at your decision? What was the result?

**Analysis:** Your intention with these types of questions is to get the candidate talking about how he or she goes about making decisions. What type of analysis does he or she use? Where does prior learning and experience fit in? Does the candidate have a track record of success? Ultimately, you want to hire a person who can and does make solid, well-thought-out decisions when faced with difficult circumstances.

223. Describe two examples of good decisions you have made in the last six months. What were the alternatives? Why were they good decisions?

224. Recall for me a time when you had to choose between several alternatives. How did you evaluate each alternative?

225. When you evaluate different choices, what are the criteria you use? Give me a specific example.

226. Tell me about the tools and techniques you use to help your decision-making process.

**Analysis:** When evaluating decision making skills, it is important to get the full picture—sometimes people claim to make difficult decisions, but when all the details are uncovered, the decision itself wasn't difficult, rather the situation was. A difficult decision is one where there are valid alternatives from which to choose. What separates a good decision maker from an average, or even poor, one is the ability to choose the best option. Listen carefully to the alternatives described, and make a judgment about the actual difficulty of the decision. Also make sure to evaluate the candidate on how he or she ends up choosing a course of action. What you want to hear is the analytical and problem-solving processes the candidate employs.

227. Tell me about the riskiest decision that you have made.

**Analysis:** Risk exponentially increases the difficulty of making a decision. Here what you are looking for is a sufficiently risky situation combined with a thorough analysis of the situation and a positive result. Risk also tends to delay decision making, so make sure to inquire about the timeline. This will enable you to determine if the candidate struck a good balance between analyzing the problem and taking action.

228. Describe a recent unpopular decision you made. How was it received? How did you handle it?

229. Tell me about a time when you made a decision and then had to justify that decision to your superiors.

230. Tell me about a time when you made a decision and then felt you had to defend your decision to coworkers or staff.

**Analysis:** These questions will help you uncover the candidate's confidence in his or her decision-making skills. It is extremely difficult to make an unpopular decision or one that is doubted. The only way the decision is successfully defended is if the analysis has been done and the alternatives clearly evaluated. What you are looking for is whether or not the candidate did dot all the "I's" and cross all the "T's." Listen for how prepared he or she was for criticism.

Another important element of this question is interpersonal skills. It is difficult to keep composure when you feel attacked or questioned. Evaluate the candidate's method for dealing with the criticism and make sure it was appropriate and professional.

231. Give me an example of a time when you had to be quick in coming to a decision.

232. What kind of decisions do you make rapidly? What kind takes more time? Give examples.

233. Describe a situation where you handled decisions under pressure or when time limits were imposed?

234. Describe a situation where a prompt and accurate decision on your part was critical. What did you consider in reaching your decision?

235. Describe a situation in which you had to draw a conclusion quickly and take speedy action.

**Analysis:** Time pressures provide a prime influence for making fair or even poor decisions. What you want to know is how much time the candidate has taken and if he or she is willing to take shortcuts with the analysis portion to come to quicker decisions. Sometimes, however, a situation calls for quick action. What you need to determine is whether the speed of the action was justified and what steps the candidate took to do a thorough analysis after the fact and/or run damage control if necessary. Quick decision making is one thing, preparing for and handling the consequences is quite another. Listen and probe for details about what happened after the decision was made and what the ultimate outcome looked like.

236. Give me an example of when taking your time to make a decision paid off.

**Analysis:** Here you want to know why the decision-making process was emphasized over the timeliness. Make sure the length of time was a result of the situation rather than the candidate's reluctance to actually make a decision.

237. Describe a time in which you weighed the pros and cons of a situation and decided not to take action, even though you were under pressure to do so?

238. Tell me about a time when you took a public stance on an issue and then had to change your position?

**Analysis:** This is another question that judges a candidate's commitment levels to their decision-making processes. Those who use a well-planned, thorough and well-executed process have no reason to second-guess themselves. What you are looking for is overall conviction as well as information about how the candidate handled the opposition. Do they continue to make efforts to keep all the stakeholders informed and satisfied, and do they handle criticism or negative feedback with professionalism?

239. Give me an example of a time when there was a decision to be made and procedures were not in place? What was the outcome?

240. Tell me about a time when you had to make a decision without all the information you needed. How did you handle it? Why? Were you happy with the outcome?

241. Give me an example of a time when you had to keep

from speaking or making a decision because you did not have enough information.

**Analysis:** While there is always a level of uncertainly in decision making, sometimes a person is forced to make a decision even when there is a glaring hole in the analysis. This is the type of question where you will be evaluating the candidate's overall experience with decision making. The process will not be thorough so the candidate needs to demonstrate how well he or she can depend on judgment and past experience to make reasonable decisions. This type of competence comes with experience, so probe to find out how often the person is confronted with situations like these and what his or her overall success rate is.

242. Tell me about a decision you made in the past that later proved to be a wrong decision. Why was it wrong? What would you do differently now, if anything, in making that decision?

243. Tell me about a situation where you made a poor decision and had to live with the consequences?

244. Give me an example of when your work contributed to making a wrong decision. What was the outcome? What, if anything, would you do differently?

**Analysis:** Accepting responsibility for a poor decision is hard, and no candidate wants to admit in an interview that he or she actually made a poor decision. However, what you need to know is how the candidate dealt with the consequences. Listen for any sign of excuses or attempts to spread the blame. What you want in an employee is someone who can stand behind good decisions as well as bad ones.

To alleviate the candidate's discomfort, shift focus to the learning process the candidate went through. Has he or she used what was learned to make future decisions? Try to determine if the setback affected the candidate's confidence. It's okay to be leery of making decisions for a while, but you don't want to hire an employee who is constantly second-guessing himself or trying to avoid important decisions altogether.

## Application: Decision-Making Skills Questions
### Applicant: Charles Davenport

### Position: Administrative Assistant

Interviewer: "Charles, can you tell me about a time when you had to make a decision very fast? What was the situation and outcome?"

Interviewee: "Oh gosh, fast decisions scare me, but I know sometimes you have no choice. Well, certainly the decision to help that employee get his vacation check was done quickly, but it turned out well in the end because I followed up on it."

Interviewer: "In our office we work with production schedules that change with sales forecasts. Sometimes that means taking whole new directions at the last minute. Can you think of an example where you had to make a decision to completely shift focus?"

Interviewee: "The only thing I can think of is when we get behind with a project. I know that I have my own tasks and responsibilities, but sometimes those have to be altered for the benefit of the department and company. In those situations I make a decision to help out my coworkers, knowing that I will be swamped later on, but the consequence is worth it."

In this situation, the interviewer recognizes quickly that Charles' experience with quick decision making is not completely relevant to the position. Since the interviewer has already had a chance to evaluate analytical and problem-solving skills, he decides to cut this section short and move on. While structured interviews are set up so that every candidate is asked the same questions, if you know that a candidate does not have relevant experience in that one area, it is futile to belabor the point.

What the interviewer did was ask the question and then use a specific work explanation in order to assist the candidate to come up with a more relevant example. Clearly, Charles has not worked in an environment that required him to make quick decisions, and that may be due to the level of responsibility and authority he has had. The interviewer knows how he makes decisions based on his answers to previous questions and it is also quite unlikely a "real" interview would examine these three interrelated competencies separately. Remember that behavioral interviews are time-consuming, so you must determine which competencies are most critical to job success, and then ask detailed questions in those specific categories.

*Focus your interview on the five or six competencies most critical for success in the position.*

# 9
# Teamwork

Working in a team environment is almost a mainstay of modern work. Whether the team is formally recognized, long-term, short-term, or simply a group of people working toward a common goal, the ability to work with others is imperative. Working within a team context is unique in that all members are equally valued, and it is the sharing of resources and expertise that makes for enhanced production. It is also a prime situation for differences in opinions, styles of work and other interpersonal issues to surface.

What you are looking for is a person who recognizes the value of teamwork and understands that to be effective, all members must collaborate. The result of this collaboration is called synergy—where the team's output is better than the performance of the strongest individual team member. Questions in the teamwork section focus on what the candidate believes to be true about effective teams and what role he or she has played on effective and ineffective teams. Look for the following:

- Recognition of what a team is.

- Understanding of synergy.

- Willingness to accept other opinions.

- Openness to different processes and procedures.

- Ability to persuade others.

- Ability to think objectively.

- Ability to motivate.

Some people mistakenly think teamwork happens when employees are willing to help each other out, cover for each other, occasionally provide input and advice, etc. True teamwork is much more complex than that and involves people working together because they truly appreciate that a collective of talents, expertise and ideas will produce superior results.

## Interview Questions for Assessing Teamwork Skills

245. Describe a time when you were a member of a team or group that had to achieve a goal or solve a problem. What type of team or group was it? What was the team or group trying to do? What was your role? How did you contribute to the team or group? Was the team or group successful?

246. Can you give me an example of a team decision you

were involved in recently? What did you do to help the team reach the decision?

247. What have you done in past situations to contribute toward a teamwork environment?

248. Describe a project you were responsible for that required a lot of interaction with people over a long period of time.

249. Tell me about a time when you had to rely on a team to get things done.

250. Describe a situation in which you were involved in a project as part of a team.

251. Describe the types of teams you've been involved with. What were your roles?

252. Describe a team experience you found rewarding.

253. Tell me about a course, work experience or extracurricular activity where you had to work closely

with others. How did it go? How did you overcome any difficulties?

254. Tell me about a time that you had to cooperate with members of other departments to solve a problem.

255. Think of a time when you worked effectively in a team situation. Describe how you felt about the contributions of the others on the team.

256. Tell me about a time when, if it hadn't been for teamwork, your goal might not have been achieved.

257. Give me an example of one of the most significant contributions you made as a member of a high-performing team. What, in your opinion, made it a high-performing team?

**Analysis:** All of these questions are designed to get the candidate talking about what being a member of a team means to him or her. Notions of teamwork are very diverse, and you need to determine if the person's experience with teamwork is adequate for your company's work environment. As mentioned, not all perceptions of teamwork are the same, so you need to figure out if the candidate will fit in well within the type of team environment evident in the company. Look for indications of the extent of teamwork; what the candidate thinks teamwork is; the candidate's idea of cooperation; what role does the candidate assume in a team situation; what qualifies as an effective team; what makes a team experience enjoyable; etc.

Listen closely for indications of the candidate's true commitment level to working in a team as well as his or her enthusiasm to do so. Most people realize that teamwork is expected, but not all people appreciate the difficulties that are involved with teamwork. Sometimes it's easier to accomplish a task on your own, but the result will not be as good as the one that an effective team accomplishes. Determine for yourself whether the candidate is "talking the talk" or if he or she "walks the walk."

258. Tell me about one of the toughest teams/groups you've had to work with. What made it difficult? What did you do?

259. Sometimes it can be frustrating when trying to get information from other people so that you can solve a problem. Please describe a situation you've had like this. What did you do?

260. Tell me about a time when you worked with a

classmate or colleague who was not doing their share of the work. How did you handle it?

261. Tell us about a time in the past year when you had to deal with a difficult team member and describe what you did.

262. Give me an example of a situation where you had difficulties with a team member. What, if anything, did you do to resolve the difficulties?

263. Tell me about a time when you had to work on a team that did not get along. What happened? What role did you take? What was the result?

264. Describe a team experience you found disappointing. What would you have done to improve the outcome?

265. Tell me about a time when you were on a team and one of the members wasn't carrying his or her weight. What did you do to try to prevent this?

**Analysis:** Teamwork is rife with conflict, disillusionment and frustration. Working closely with other people who have different values, styles, expertise, experience, perceptions, work ethics, etc., is very difficult. What you need to determine is what triggers frustration in the candidate and what he or she does to get over it. Listen for the use of interpersonal and conflict-resolutions skills that preserve a professional working environment but that make sure everyone in the team is heard and understood.

Be alert for clues that might indicate the candidate is more the cause of the conflict than part of the solution. These people typically discuss what other people did and take little or no responsibility for the difficulty. They concentrate their answers on what went wrong and may even express disgust or disdain for the actions of others. Effective team members present conflict as a shared dynamic and focus more on the solutions than the problems.

266. Give me an example of when you were on a team that failed to meet its objectives. What could the team have done differently?

**Analysis:** This question is designed to get the candidate to think objectively about the team's overall performance. Make sure the candidate takes adequate responsibility for the failure and discusses his or her performance and how it contributed to the ineffectiveness. What you don't want is a candidate who focuses on what other people did wrong and maintains a righteous view of the situation. Also look for indications that the candidate espouses a team approach when discussing what should have been done differently. You'd be surprised at the number of people who will say things like, "If they had done it the way I'd suggested..." as part of their answer to the solution.

267. Gaining the cooperation of others can be difficult. Give a specific example of when you had to do that and what challenges you faced. What was the outcome? What was the long-term impact on your ability to work with this person?

268. Describe how you felt about a decision the team wanted to make that you didn't agree with.

269. Describe a situation where the team was having trouble agreeing on a decision and what you did to facilitate consensus.

270. Describe a situation where others you were working with on a project disagreed with your ideas. What did you do?

271. Describe a situation in which you had to arrive at a compromise or help others to compromise. What was your role? What steps did you take? What was the result?

**Analysis:** One of the main challenges of working within a team is getting and maintaining cooperation. The whole idea of teamwork is to bring together different opinions and perspectives in the hopes of creating a better outcome than any one person could come up with. These interpersonal differences are what make coming to a consensus so difficult. What you are evaluating is the candidate's appreciation of these differences and what strategies he or she uses to handle the mixture constructively. Of particular interest is the role the individual plays in the situation. Do they tend toward mediator, reconciliatory, judge, compiler, evaluator, etc.? Evaluate the answer in terms of fit with the current team as well as appropriateness of the role.

272. Tell me about a time where you were a member of a team and had to encourage everyone to participate.

273. Give me an example of something you did that helped build enthusiasm in others.

**Analysis:** With these inquiries, you are trying to determine how much spirit and enthusiasm the candidate brings to a team situation. Some people are very comfortable in a motivational or inspirational role and others are not. Use this information to again evaluate overall fit with the current team and demands of the role.

274. Tell me about a team where you were the leader. How did you promote the effectiveness of your team? What were the results?

275. When dealing with individuals or groups, how do you determine when you are pushing too hard?

**Analysis:** Use these questions if the candidate is applying for a role that is expected to take on a leadership role within a team. While most teams have specified leaders, it is also true that some people emerge as a leader due to their expertise or experience and will fluctuate between roles depending on the project. Listen for signs of leadership but with a definite tendency toward egalitarian methods of gaining cooperation and buy-in. An autocratic leadership style is not conducive to teamwork, so make sure to evaluate the fit and appropriateness.

## Application: Teamwork Skills Questions
**Applicant: Charles Davenport**

**Position: Administrative Assistant**

Interviewer:     "We work as a team in our office with everyone pitching in and helping out. Occasionally we also work on larger projects that require a team effort. Can you tell me about a project-specific team that you worked on?"

Interviewee:     "Sure, it was when we were putting together the new policy and procedure manual. There were four of us working on the project—we needed to get input from the various departments to make sure the policies made sense and were actually practical. The whole reason for the revamp was because some of the policies were out of date and others were not even relevant. We met every week for a month and a half, and we each had our own responsibilities that we put together to create the finished manual. It was a lot of work and I know I couldn't have done as thorough a job if it was just myself and my boss working on it."

Interviewer:     "What role did you take on within the team?"

Interviewee:     "Well, at first I was kind of the leader. It was my overall responsibility to complete the manual but whomever had the most expertise in the area we were discussing ended up being the leader for that section. Because we all had very different experiences with the manual, and reasons for wanting it updated, it worked out well."

Interviewer:     "Can you tell me about any conflicts you had during the process, how it was resolved, and what the outcome was?"

Interviewee:     "The conflicts were a result of our differences in focus. Because I'm part of the admin group, my main concern was clarity and ease of use, while the other people were more concerned about the specifics of the policy and how it would affect the department or specific jobs, so we had a few heated discussions about wording and relevance, but one person in the group was always able to take the role of mediator and help us work through it. I think what made it such a strong team was that not everyone had a strong interest in every section so there was always someone who could be objective and help set the priorities."

Interviewer:     "What I'd like is some detail on a specific conflict you were faced with and how you handled it."

Interviewee:     "Well, this other guy and I were at odds a few times over quality of work. Like I said, we each had certain responsibilities that we were expected to complete for each meeting. This guy was obviously completing his stuff minutes before the meeting and it was sloppy, unorganized and incomplete. Because this was a team effort, I thought we should discus it as a team. At the beginning of the next meting I added "quality of work" to the agenda and opened the topic up to comments. Everyone else had the same problem with the guy, so I didn't have to be the bad guy, and peer pressure worked to get him to improve his reports and assignments. It worked out really well."

Interviewer: "So, in a team environment when there is conflict between two members, how do you deal with it?"

Interviewee: "I think that it is up to them to deal with the problem directly. If you have a problem with someone, you should be able to discuss it openly and work it out. That's what we did with the guy who was doing sloppy work and it worked out."

What we see in this scenario is the interviewer probing to affirm what he already suspected about the candidate's interpersonal skills. Charles' answers were quite vague and general, so he was prompted to provide specifics. What he revealed was confirmation that he does not deal with conflict directly but gets others to intervene. In this case he made a personal issue part of a team meeting in hopes that others would deal with the issue and allow him to avoid the responsibility.

The interview used a final probe to get Charles' opinion about dealing with interpersonal conflict and he again slipped into a generalization that was in line with what we are "told" is the right way to deal with conflict. What this proves is that behavioral interviewing is the key to finding out what a candidate really does, rather than what they know they should do. Remember to probe for as much specific detail as you need to uncover a candidate's actual behavior. If the candidate tries to generalize or give opinions when you want real examples, gently but firmly ask for specifics. You might have to ask a few times, but make sure you persist. As you can see, real examples will reveal the most insightful and relevant information.

*Continue to probe for specific details that will confirm your opinion about a candidate's competency in a certain area.*

# 10
# Organization

An efficient employee is an organized one. The ability to establish a course of action for yourself (and/or others) is essential for accomplishing goals thoroughly and on time. Organization requires proper planning of assignments and allocating resources. Time spent organizing and planning will ensure steps are not missed, timelines are met, and tasks are prioritized. To be well organized, a person must employ particular tools and techniques. Look for evidence that the candidate uses a variety of strategies to remain focused. Examples include:

- Daytimer

- Planning calendars

- To-do lists

- Flow charts

- Visual planning software (e.g.,. GAANT charts)

- Timelines

- Scheduling software

- Whiteboards

- Filing systems

- Regular meetings

What you are looking for is examples of when these types of tools have been used and how well they have helped the candidate improve the efficiency and completeness of his or her work. Evaluate the candidate's answer on how well and often they use organizational tools, how well they prioritize tasks, and how they deal with deadlines. The purpose of organization is to avoid the stress and pressure associated with time crunches and procrastination, so make sure these are not problem areas for the candidate.

## Interview Questions for Assessing Organization Skills

276. Are you able to schedule your time? How far ahead can you schedule?

277. Can you walk me through last week and tell me how you planned the week's activities and how the schedule worked out?

278. How do you schedule your time? Set priorities?

279. Describe a time in school when you had many projects

or assignments due at the same time. What steps did you take to get them all done?

280. What have you done in order to be effective with your organization and planning?

281. Give me an example of when your ability to manage your time and priorities proved to be an asset.

282. Tell me about a project that you planned. How did you organize and schedule the tasks? Tell me about your action plan.

**Analysis:** With these questions you are establishing the candidate's preference for and use of organizational tools. Which tools does the candidate use? Evaluate whether or not the tool is sufficient for the magnitude of the project. While a to-do list might be adequate for a project with a timeline of a few days, large projects require schedules and timelines and other long-term planning tools. Try to find evidence that the candidate uses a variety of planning tools and is flexible enough to adapt to the situation at hand.

Another avenue to explore is how much time the candidate spends planning. Neglecting the planning phase is detriment to productivity but so is over-planning. People who plan every detail may have trouble adapting to changes in schedules, priorities, etc., and may spend more time organizing their work than actually doing their work. If you have doubts, use probes to determine if the candidate strikes a healthy balance between the two extremes.

283. Describe a time when you had to handle multiple responsibilities and how you managed it.

284. How do you handle doing twenty things at once?

285. We often have multiple tasks to accomplish in a day. Tell me about a time when you had to handle many competing priorities. How did you plan your time? What were the results?

286. Describe a situation that required things to be done at the same time. How did you handle the situation? What was the result?

287. How do you prioritize projects and tasks when scheduling your time? Give me some examples. How do you determine priorities in scheduling your time? Give me an example.

288. Tell me about a time when you were particularly effective at prioritizing tasks and completing a project on schedule.

289. If you are faced with two pressing projects and only have time to complete one, how will you decide which one to complete? Try to use an example from real life.

290. How do you decide what gets top priority when scheduling your time?

291. How do you determine priorities in scheduling your time? Give examples.

**Analysis:** With this line of questioning what you are trying to determine is whether or not the candidate is willing and able to prioritize. When there are competing tasks and deadlines it is very difficult to determine which projects get worked on and when. What you want to hear about are specific situations when the candidate had to prioritize tasks and on what basis the determination was made. Without any express planning and forethought, often the more enjoyable or easier tasks are worked on. What you want to know is how the candidate goes about filling his or her work schedule. What considerations are made for competing deadlines and large workloads?

292. We all have had times when we just couldn't get everything done on time. Tell me about a time when this has happened to you.

293. We have all had occasions when we were working on something that just "slipped through the cracks." Can you give me some examples of when this happened to you and what were the results?

294. At one time or another we've all forgotten to do something important for a customer. Tell me about a time this happened to you recently. What did you forget? Why? What happened?

**Analysis:** Even the most diligent of planners will miss a deadline or forget to do something. What you are interested in is what circumstances led to the mistake and then how the situation was corrected. The purpose of asking this question is not to embarrass the candidate or make him or her feel uncomfortable, so make sure you put more emphasis on the final outcome and what was learned. What you are trying to determine is how the candidate's experience has made him or her a better organizer or planner.

295. Has your time schedule ever been upset by unforeseen circumstances? Give me a recent example. What did you do then?

296. Tell me about a situation you observed or were a part of where there were time and/or resource constraints. What happened? Why?

**Analysis:** The best-laid plans are inevitably put to the test. What you want to know is whether or not the candidate anticipates this type of change. Does he or she build in contingency plans or extra time to accommodate change? Listen carefully for how well the candidate prepared for and then dealt with the unforeseen circumstance. Probe for more examples and determine how well the candidate responds to change in general.

297. What objectives did you set for this year? What steps have you taken to make sure you're making progress on all of them?

**Analysis:** This question deals with a candidate's ability and willingness to set long-range plans for himself or herself. It is not uncommon for employees to get too task-oriented and their planning calendars are just a long laundry list of to-do items. A candidate who recognizes the power of planning will use those same tools to set professional goals. What you are looking for is whether or not the candidate takes a more strategic outlook to their day-to-day tasks and sees how his or her accomplishments fit into the company's big picture.

298. Tell me about a time when you were given a deadline by someone of higher authority which could not possibly be met. How did you handle it?

299. Tell me about the last project you worked on that had a fixed deadline.

300. Describe for me a time when you missed a deadline. What was the result and what did you learn from the experience?

301. Can you tell me about a time when you rushed the completion of a project, sacrificing quality for efficiency?

**Analysis:** Deadlines are inevitable and can be stress inducing if you don't plan adequately for full completion of a project. What you want to know is how well the candidate responds to deadlines and what factors contributed to missed deadlines. Of equal importance is the recognition that quality and completion should not be rushed just to make a deadline. Communication is important in all projects, and you should look for evidence that the candidate keeps all stakeholders informed about the progress and status of a project. This type of process will more often result in modified deadlines rather than missed ones.

302. Give me an example of when you were able to meet the personal and professional demands in your life yet still maintained a healthy balance.

303. Describe a time when you had to make a difficult choice between your personal and professional life.

*Planning and organization will help a person maintain balance but, ultimately, personal and professional lives will collide.*

**Analysis:** This is an interesting line of questioning that helps you determine overall fit with the company and its values and ideals. Of course, a balanced lifestyle is the ultimate goal but some workplaces have more of an emphasis on this than

169

others. If your workplace is fast-paced, go, go, go, then you need employees who are willing to sacrifice their personal life for certain periods of time or under certain circumstances, and the opposite is true as well. Planning and organization will help a person maintain balance but, ultimately, personal and professional lives will collide. You have to use your best judgment to determine a candidate's fit with your company.

304. Tell me about a time when you needed to keep a wide variety of people updated or informed on an on-going basis. What steps or process did you use to accomplish your task? What were the results?

**Analysis:** With this question you are evaluating the communication processes a candidate builds into his or her overall project plan. As mentioned in another question, keeping stakeholders up to date on your progress is the best way to ensure no one is surprised with a result. Look for specific evidence that the candidate plans to communicate and then follows through with the communication. Determine whether the communicating method used was appropriate and sufficient, and question the candidate about how well the information was received and understood (refer to the communication skills section for more ideas).

## Application: Organization Skills Questions
### Applicant: Charles Davenport

### Position: Administrative Assistant

Interviewer: "Needless to say, the job of an administrative assistant requires excellent planning and organization skills. Tell me how you planned your last week of work."

Interviewee: "Typically what I do is sit down with my boss every Monday morning and we review what needs to be done. I make notes and then plan out my week's activities. What I like to do is use a Daytimer that has all the days of the week on one open page. That way I know what is coming up and what to prepare for."

Interviewer: "What exact types of activities do you track in your Daytimer?"

Interviewee: "I use it to write deadlines or meetings or when certain projects are supposed to be complete. I like to have those reminders so I don't forget to do something important or miss a deadline or meeting or something."

Interviewer: "Well, that brings me to my next question. Can

you describe for me a time when you did miss a deadline? What happened and what was the result?"

Interviewee: "Well, it doesn't happen very often but a few months ago when we were in the final stages of putting together that new policy and procedure manual, I was a few days late submitting our employee's benefit claims. The project was in my Daytimer so I did plan to complete it but unfortunately I got so busy that I didn't even see it. I was concentrating so heavily on my other project. Thankfully, I was able to call and fax the claims directly to the person responsible for processing, and she was able to process the requests on time. What I've done since then is use bright yellow highlighter to mark each of my deadlines and other important dates in my Daytimer. I can't miss the yellow and it leaps up at me from the page every week."

Interviewer: "Besides your Daytimer, do you use any other planning tools on a regular basis?"

Interviewee: "No, not really. My Daytimer is really all I need. It works for me and now that I can't miss seeing my deadlines, I haven't had a problem. I am a naturally very organized person—you should see my desk—so my Daytimer is my way of backing up the information that I store in my brain."

Interviewer: "Can you relate for me a time when you had to cut corners in order to complete a project on time?"

Interviewee: "I'm not the type who cuts corners. There are times when I realize I didn't get everything done in a day that needed to be done so I just stay late and complete the work properly. I am very committed to my job and I will put in whatever time is necessary to complete the job properly. I have a strong work ethic, and I don't see myself ever being able to sacrifice quality for speed."

The interviewer sets up this section with a note about how important organizational skills are to the job for which the candidate is applying. When the candidate doesn't provide enough information in response to the first question, the interviewer asks specifically for more details. The interviewer immediately recognizes a flaw in the candidate's organizational skills—he relies on a Daytimer to plan deadlines and major events but there is no daily task planning or prioritization mentioned, so the interviewer probes further to make sure this initial evaluation is valid. When the interviewer receives confirmation that the candidate has only one organizational tool, his red-flag concerns are confirmed.

The warning signs were there, and the interviewer capitalized on the situation making sure to provide the candidate with more opportunities to fully explain his planning techniques. With this interview, it is interesting to note that the last question in the section affirms why effective planning is so important. If the candidate did use a daily to-do list or some other prioritization process, he would not have to stay late to complete work. Use each section of the interview to confirm or deny opinions you've formed and evaluations you've made. The more supporting evidence you can gather for your final decision, the more confident you will be when making the decision.

*Use each section of interview questions to confirm or deny previous evaluations you have made.*

# 11
## Motivation

An employee's motivation is one of the most important factors in employee productivity. A paycheck only motivates to a certain degree; after that, other factors need to be present to drive an employee to perform good work. Those other factors are the activities and responsibilities that provide personal satisfaction as well as job satisfaction. What you are looking for is an employee who is motivated to do a good job because he or she derives intrinsic satisfaction from knowing that a job was done well.

Signs that an employee is internally motivated to do good work and accomplish high levels of productivity include:

- Active goal setting.

- Understanding how their role fits into the big picture.

- Determination.

- Persistence.

- Participation in professional development.

- Willingness to learn new things.

- Positive approach to challenges.

- Task initiation rather than acceptance.

- Providing a positive influence in the workplace.

What you need to assess in this section is how likely the candidate is to need external rewards and other forms of explicit recognition in order to do a good job. Obviously, what you want is an employee who is self-motivated to do excellent work and who does not accept any less, regardless of the accolades received or recognition given. Ultimately you will have to evaluate the fit of the candidate's motivation needs with the motivational elements provided by the company.

## Interview Questions for Assessing Motivation

305. Tell me about an important goal that you set in the past. Were you successful? Why?

306. Give me an example of the most significant professional goal you have met. How did you achieve it? What were the obstacles? How did you overcome them?

307. Give me an example of when you have worked the hardest and felt the greatest sense of achievement.

308. Give me an example of an important goal that you have set in the past, and tell me about your success in reaching it.

309. Give me an example of when you took a risk to achieve a goal. What was the outcome?

310. What are your future professional goals? How do you plan to achieve them? What might keep you from achieving them?

311. Tell me about a time when you set and achieved a goal.

312. What were your objectives for last year? Were they achieved? How?

313. Tell me about a performance standard that you have set for yourself. How are you working towards meeting that standard?

314. Tell me about a time when you overcame great obstacles to achieve something significant.

**Analysis:** With these questions you are trying to determine how goal-oriented the candidate is as well as how likely he or she is to actually set goals for himself or herself. Some people are very good at achieving goals that are set for them, but those people who actively set their own goals are the ones who are continuously striving to improve and perform at higher levels than expected. On the other hand, you want to be sure that the candidate is not the type who sets goals but doesn't actually follow through with them. Make sure you get a complete picture of the goal-setting process as well as the result.

The other portion of these questions you need to consider is how the person actually tracks his or her progress. This is another valuable indicator of how motivated the person is by goal setting. Evaluate how well the candidate keeps track of his or her goals and whether there are intermediate steps along the way that are recognized as achievements. Highly motivated individuals use these short-term accomplishments to bolster their drive to the end.

315. Describe a situation when you were able to have a positive influence on the actions of others.

316. Relate a scenario where you were responsible for motivating others.

317. Describe a situation when you were able to have a positive influence on the action of others.

**Analysis:** Motivating yourself is one thing, motivating others is quite another. What you want to know is whether the candidate is able to remain upbeat and enthusiastic about company-wide goals and if that enthusiasm is infectious. Use these inquiries to determine if the candidate is likely to take on a "championing" role within your organization and help motivate others to accomplish company-wide objectives.

318. How would you define "success" for someone in your chosen career?

319. What are your standards of success in your job/school? What have you done to meet these standards?

320. In your position, how do you define doing a good job?

**Analysis:** This question will provide invaluable clues into what motivates the candidate to perform at an exemplary level. Use the answer to determine if the candidate is more or less motivated by extrinsic factors than intrinsic ones. The employees who will require less maintenance and attention are the ones who use internal feelings of satisfaction and pride to gauge when a job has been performed successfully. Listen for examples where the candidate did not receive external recognition but still knew he or she was successful.

321. Give an example of when your persistence had the biggest payoff. Give me an example of when you achieved something by your persistence that others couldn't.

322. Please describe a time when you were successful at an activity only after repeated attempts.

323. Describe a situation in which you persevered with an idea or a plan even when others disagreed with you.

**Analysis:** Persistence in the face of challenge or adversity is the mark of a highly motivated individual. What you need to determine is whether that persistence is channeled in an appropriate manner. There are people who persevere even when the end result is so longer valid or relevant. These people, though highly motivated, are misguided and may not be the most productive people on your team. What you need to determine is whether the persistence paid off in terms of benefit to the company or benefit to the individual. What you want is an employee who works tirelessly to achieve corporate objectives and doesn't lose sight of the overall goal just to prove a point or meet a personal challenge.

324. Give examples of your experiences at school or in a job that were satisfying.

325. For what kind of supervisor do you work best? Provide examples.

326. Give me an example of a time when a project really excited you.

327. Tell me about the things you like about your current or most recent job.

328. Under what conditions do you work best?

**Analysis:** These questions are designed to uncover what external factors the candidate considers motivating. Self-motivation is wonderful but we all need to work in an environment that is pleasing and enjoyable. Figure out what it is about a situation that makes it satisfying for the candidate, and then compare those characteristics to what the workplace offers and determine if there is a good fit. Since motivation is one of the keys to productivity, you are best to start off with employees who will find your company a desirable place to work.

329. Tell me about a time when you were given an assignment that was distasteful or unpleasant.

330. Tell me what your least favorite part or parts are of your current or most recent job.

331. Your supervisor asks you to complete a task that you cannot stand doing. How do you react to him or her?

**Analysis:** It's easy to get motivated by a project or situation that is interesting and exciting, but the true test of one's motivation is how one reacts when the circumstances are less than inviting. The purpose of these questions is twofold: determine what the candidate dislikes and how he or she reacts to an undesirable situation. It is good to know upfront what duties or circumstances are unpleasant for a candidate and then evaluate the likelihood of encountering those situations in your workplace. More people leave positions for reasons of fit than all other reasons combined, so it is critical to make sure the candidate you hire has a fighting chance from the start.

The other aspect is, of course, how the candidate approaches situations that are least favorable. Every job carries a certain number of elements that are less than optimum, and you need to determine if the candidate approaches these tasks with negativity and disdain or if he or she is able to dig "way down deep" and find something motivating about the situation even if it is just the thought of finishing.

332. When was a time that you were most dissatisfied with
    your work?

333. All jobs have their frustrations and problems. Describe
    some examples of specific job conditions, tasks or
    assignments that have been dissatisfying to you.

334. Give examples of your experiences that were
    dissatisfying.

**Analysis:** What you are trying to evaluate with this type of
question is how the candidate reacts to and recovers from
disappointment or dissatisfaction. Again, we are talking about
attitude, and what you are looking for is a genuine ability to see
the positive in any situation. Look for candidates who focus
more on what they learned from the experience and are able to
see the benefit of the situation. Those who concentrate on the
negative aspects of the situation tend to be stuck in the
negative and are not as likely to motivate themselves to recover,
learn and move on.

335. Describe a really tough or long day and how you dealt
    with the situation?

336. How have you motivated yourself to complete an assignment or task that you did not want to do?

337. Describe a time when you were unmotivated to get a job done?

338. Have you found any ways to make school or a job easier or more rewarding?

**Analysis:** These are direct questions designed to uncover a candidate's ability to self-motivate. You will learn what the candidate values and feels is important for his or her own satisfaction. Evaluate your work environment against those factors to determine the level of fit for the organization. Certainly anyone who is successful at self-motivation is well suited to most positions, but the better the overall fit, the better the chances of developing a long-term employee.

339. Describe a situation where you were asked to assume responsibility for something you had never handled before.

**Analysis:** Here is a question that involves motivation and confidence. Answers you want to hear are ones that include some trepidation but overall excitement and honor at being given the responsibility. High motivation levels are excellent but they have to be kept in check by a realistic sense of what one is and is not capable of doing with the skills and resources available. Look for answers that include seeking outside assistance and expertise to complete the task as well as the typical strategies of goal setting and intrinsic rewards. There is a fine line between being motivated and "up" for anything and biting off more than one can chew. It is your job to determine if the person in front of you has a healthy respect and understanding of his or her own abilities and limits.

## Application: Motivation Questions
### Applicant: Charles Davenport

### Position: Administrative Assistant

Interviewer: "Charles, I'd like to switch gears a bit and get to know a little more about you and specifically what you find motivating."

Interviewee: "I love responsibility. I am really motivated when I know my boss trusts me to complete my work and doesn't feel the need to check up on me or hover over me. Not that I don't take direction well, because I do. I just work my best when the onus is more on me to ask for questions and clarification rather than my boss assuming I need help or assistance when I don't. I think I'm also like a lot of other people in that I like to hear that I'm doing a good job or that my work is appreciated. No one needs to take out a big ad in the paper but a genuine 'thank you' every once in a while certainly makes we want to work extra hard."

Interviewer: "So, tell me about the last time you felt really unmotivated to do something."

Interviewee: "Well, I guess every month when I know the filing has to be caught up I cringe a little inside. It's not my favorite task but I know it has to be done so I set up a little competition with myself. I went to my boss with the idea when I realized I was letting the filing slip more and more. I set a time that I have to have all the filing done—there are no excuses and no second chances—if I get it done in time, I can come to work 30 minutes later one day in the next month. We've been doing it for over a year and I only missed one month."

Interviewer: "Describe for me the things you have liked about your workplaces."

Interviewee: "As I said before, responsibility and autonomy are really important. It's also important that the people in the office are respectful and professional. We had a receptionist for a while that was rude and foul-mouthed and it really brought the whole office morale down, so pleasant people are important. And it may sound silly but it's important that the office be clean. When I was in college I temped at a few places that were dirty and it really turned me off. For me to do a good job I need to know that the boss or owner takes as much pride in his operation as I do in my work."

Interviewer:       "Our office is based on the team approach, so I would like to hear about a situation where you motivated others to complete an assignment or do a good job."

Interviewee:       "I think I motivate others just with my optimism and positive outlook. I really try not to bring negativity into the workplace and I know others see me as a role model, of sorts, when it comes to the right attitude for the job."

Interviewer:       "Can you describe a specific situation where you did something overt, or beyond just displaying a positive attitude, to motivate someone else?"

Interviewee:    "I guess what I do is use a lot of praise and encouragement and try to pay extra attention to the person in order to cheer them up. Like last week our receptionist was feeling down because her husband had left on a three-week business trip. What I did was invite her to dinner with my wife and I one night and I also made sure to be extra helpful and appreciative of the things she did. After the first week, I noticed her attitude changed and she thanked me for being so considerate. That felt good."

This section is very insightful. The interviewer is discovering more personal aspects of Charles' personality and preferences which will allow him to make a valid assessment of Charles' ability to fit into the company culture. Notice that she starts off with an opinion question rather than a behavioral one. This is a deliberate attempt to get Charles thinking about what motivates him. Often we are unaware of our motivations so it helps to stimulate the thought process early on in the questions in order to avoid weak or incomplete answers later.

You'll also notice that Charles has more difficulty with this line of questioning than the others and, again, that is likely because motivation is a competence that has an ethereal quality to it. It's hard for a candidate to give a specific answer to what he or she finds motivational, so it is your job to pull the information out of him or her with effective, and perhaps numerous, probes. It is common for candidates to revert to opinions and generalizations when the questions get a little deep and personal. That's okay; just make sure you are prepared to probe further, and don't relent until you get the information you need.

The final issue to consider with competencies that are considered essential to most jobs is the candidate's anticipation of these exact questions. Charles did offer responses that could be considered canned, pre-prepared or even coached. Always be leery of generalizations, and make sure you insist on getting detailed, specific examples of times when the competency was actually demonstrated. Be understanding of the candidate's unfamiliarity with behavioral interviewing but don't let up until you have an answer with which you are satisfied.

*Be on the lookout for canned or coached answers, and insist on specific, detailed examples for all of your behavioral questions.*

*Initiative is generally what separates an average employee from an exceptional one.*

# 12

# Initiative

Initiative is often confused with motivation, and although the two competencies are related, they are unique. Initiative refers to an employee's ability to be a self-starter and see work without explicit directions or prompts. Initiative is generally what separates an average employee from an exceptional one. The average person satisfies the job description, and the exceptional one sees it as a starting point for future responsibility.

You want to hire people with initiative because you know and trust that task will be accomplished with minimal levels of supervision and direction. Highly self-directed employees understand how their roles fit into the mission and vision of the company and they find ways to enhance the company with every task or project they take on. Characteristics to look for include:

- Proactive

- Capable

- Risk-taker

- Visionary

- Dedicated

- Strategic

Your goal with these questions is to determine how well the candidate recognizes the importance of going beyond what is expected and doing what is needed. There is no room for "that's not in my job description" comments, so you have to be diligent in determining how far above and beyond the call of duty the applicant is really willing and able to go.

## Interview Questions for Assessing Initiative

340. What did you do to prepare for this interview?

**Analysis:** Here is a question most candidates are not expecting—they expect to be asked what they know about the company but not what they did to prepare. The beauty of it is the fact that you can easily verify if they did what they claimed by asking for a few facts they should have uncovered.

Aside from the element of surprise, this question is an ultimate initiative question. How much further than checking out the company Web site did the candidate actually go to understand what the company was about? A candidate with a strong answer to this question almost qualifies for an "Advance to 'GO' and collect $200 (or get the job)" card.

341. Give an example of a time when you went above and beyond the call of duty.

342. Tell me about some projects you generated on your own. What prompted you to begin them?

343. Tell me about a time when you did more than was expected of you.

344. Give me an example of a time when you were given a project and did more than was required in order to exceed someone's expectation.

345. Describe a time when you decided on your own that something needed to be done, and you took on the task to get it done.

346. Give me examples of projects/tasks you started on your own.

347. How have you demonstrated initiative? Tell me about a time when you demonstrated the most initiative.

348. Tell me about a project you initiated. What did you do? Why? What was the outcome? Were you happy with the result?

349. What have you done in your present/previous job that went beyond what was required?

**Analysis:** These classic initiative prompts will provide valuable information about what specific activities a candidate feels are "above and beyond the call of duty." Some people think taking his or her coffee of cup to the sink is a stretch, while others stay late, pick up the slack, identify new projects, etc. You need to evaluate whether the candidate's idea of initiative and supporting examples are worthy of being considered exceptional.

350. Describe for me two improvements you have made in your job in the past six months.

351. Describe any significant project ideas, etc., you have initiated or thought of in the past year. How did you know they were needed and would work? Where they used? Do they work?

352. Give me an example of time when you made a suggestion that would improve operations, either through cost cutting, increasing profits, steamlining a system, etc.

353. What have you done in the past that demonstrates your commitment to continuous improvement?

354. What proactive steps have you taken to make your workplace more efficient and productive? Specifically describe a policy, project or system you created or initiated.

355. Tell me about a suggestion you made to improve the way job processes/operations worked. What was the result?

356. Tell me about a time when you improved the way things were typically done on the job.

357. Describe something you have done to improve the performance of your work unit.

358. Describe something you have done to maximize or

improve the use of resources beyond your own work unit to achieve improved results.

359. Describe how you have improved the productivity of your most recent assignment.

**Analysis:** Many employees do what they do the way they do it because that's the way it's been done for years and years. An employee with initiative and drive will think critically about the way things operate and come up with suggestions to improve efficiency, productivity or both. Employees who see how things ought to be done are the type of people who that make positive contributions to the workplace.

360. What are some of the best ideas you have ever sold to a superior? What was your approach?

361. Describe some projects or ideas (not necessarily your own) that were implemented or carried out successfully primarily because of your efforts.

362. Tell me about a time when your initiative caused a change to occur.

363. Give me an example of a situation that could not have happened successfully without you being there.

364. What was the best idea you came up with during your professional or college career? How did you apply it?

**Analysis:** This is your opportunity to determine how useful the candidate's suggestions for improvement really were. There is a difference between constructive change and changing simply for the sake of it. Your job is to determine how practical and well founded the candidate's ideas and plans were. You don't necessarily want someone who is too radical or intent on transformation unless that is the sort of work environment your company encourages.

365. Tell me about a situation where you attempted to improve something and you were met with resistance. How did you handle the situation?

**Analysis:** These negative situation questions are always very revealing. You need to get a complete understanding of the situation and then try to understand what exactly about the idea was poorly received. Perhaps it was premature or not well planned or maybe the consequences weren't fully explored; whatever the reason, what you want to know is how the candidate dealt with the reaction and how it impacted his or her motivation to initiate projects in the future. Be sure to explore what the candidate learned from the situation and how it impacted the process used to evaluate and present other new ideas.

366. Give some instances in which you anticipated problems and were able to influence a new direction.

367. Describe a situation in which you recognized a potential problem as an opportunity. What did you do? What was the result? What do you wish you had done differently?

**Analysis:** Often initiative is born out of necessity, and while the average employee will sit back and let the boss deal with problems down the road, the employee who is driven and sees the big picture will recognize the opportunity and devise a plan to address it. What you want to know is how successfully the candidate developed a proactive solution to a problem before it even became a problem. Candidates who provide solid answers to these types of questions deserve serious consideration; however, recognize that not all interviewees will be able to come up with appropriate or relevant answers. Work with what you get and make the best evaluation you can.

## Application: Initiative Questions
**Applicant: Charles Davenport**

**Position: Administrative Assistant**

Interviewer: "We were just talking about motivation, and now I'd like to focus on initiative. Please tell me what initiative means to you."

Interviewee: "Initiative means seeing work that has to be done and doing it without having to be asked."

Interviewer: "Give me an example in the last week where you demonstrated initiative."

Interviewee: "It's kind of silly but around our office it is really a big deal. We don't have a coffee service so we supply our own coffee and make it in the company's perk. By the end of the week it is an atrocious mess and, like I said, I hate dirty workplaces so I often take it upon myself to clean it up midweek before the cleaning company comes in on the weekends. It doesn't take much time and it is a good way for me to use my spare time, when I have any. I often go out of my way to do little things like that around the office that no one else thinks to do."

Interviewer: "Can you describe for me a time when you suggested an improvement in a process or system that was implemented by the company?"

Interviewee: "Well, that whole policy and procedure manual update was my suggestion. Since I'm the one who deals with most of the forms, I realized that the information on lots of them was no longer relevant. I knew it would be an involved task but I also knew there would be a lot of time-saving once all the new policies were in place. So I went to my boss and explained the situation, she had me present the idea to the owner and he agreed it was time for a revamp so we went ahead and did it. I actually got a lot of positive feedback about the new manual and many people said they had the same idea but never wanted to tackle such a large task."

Interviewer: "Tell me about a suggestion you made that wasn't well-received or implemented. How did you feel and what did you do?"

Interviewee: "You know, I don't think there ever was a time that I made a suggestion that wasn't implemented. I'm pretty good at analyzing the outcome and all the possible problems before I make a suggestion. If anything, I guess I'm cautious. I see where change is necessary, but unless I'm pretty sure my idea has merit, I don't talk about it."

Interviewer:     "Tell me about some ideas you've had that you haven't presented."

Interviewee:     "I did want to revamp the payroll system. We use such a manual process and I thought we could improve it. I sat on the idea for a few months and then my boss announced that we were getting a new software system for payroll and all human resource functions. Whether my idea would have sped up the process, I'm not sure, but I know I wasn't in a position to suggest a new software system because changes that involve that kind of money are left up to management."

Interviewer:     "Tell me more about that. What other sorts of decisions are best left to management?"

Interviewee:     "Certainly anything to do with significant amounts of money. Other decisions include staffing. I wanted to suggest the sales department get some part-time help a long time before they did, but I kept quiet about my helping them because I didn't think it was my place to say anything. I try to go to my boss when I'm having difficulty with another employee—the whole discipline and performance area is another thing left for management. Some people are so belligerent that the only ones who will get through to them are mangers."

Charles's answers to the first part of this section are very impressive, but he opens the door to some close examination of his beliefs and perspectives on management vs. staff roles. It seems Charles' reliance on management to solve interpersonal issues stems from his deep-rooted sense that that is their job. This may or may not be an attitude you choose to work with, but the interviewer was very astute and probed for more details even though her questions deviated from the realm of initiative. It is important not to get so focused on your questions that you miss opportunities to get impromptu bits of information that reveal more about a candidate than any prepared question could.

The whole idea of interviewing is that it is a structured conversation. Keep in mind that the structure comes from standard questions; the conversation element relies on a natural flow of questions and answers. If the candidate is heading in the wrong direction, reel him or her in; if the candidate heads into a different direction than expected, evaluate the usefulness of the information and proceed as appropriate. No information is bad information; your job is to extract the most relevant information, and if a candidate offers something that is potentially beneficial, you need to be flexible enough to capitalize on the situation.

*Remain flexible throughout the interview and be open to probing for information outside the competency being investigated.*

*Some stress is motivating, yet too much stress can be debilitating, not to mention a serious health concern.*

# 13
# Stress Management

Stress and pressure are in abundance in today's workplace, and the presence of either often brings out employees' worst behaviors, habits and attitudes. Some stress is motivating, yet too much stress can be debilitating, not to mention a serious health concern. What you, as the interviewer, need to assess is whether the candidate has developed mechanisms to cope with stress and whether the strategies are successful.

Some of the more common stress-management tools to be aware of include:

- Identifying stress triggers.

- Eliminating stressors.

- Reducing the intensity of emotional reactions to stress.

- Moderating physical reactions to stress.

- Building physical reserves.

- Maintaining emotional reserves.

Be aware that most people know what they should do manage stress in their lives; your job is to determine if they actually can and do manage it.

## Interview Questions for Assessing Stress-Management Skills

368. Tell me about a high-stress situation when it was desirable for you to keep a positive attitude.

369. Tell me about a decision you made while under a lot of pressure.

370. Narrate a situation in which you experienced a particularly high level of stress.

371. Describe a time where you were faced with problems or stresses that tested your coping skills.

372. Give me an example of a high-pressure situation you have faced this past year and how you resolved it.

373. Describe a time when you were in a high-pressure situation.

374. Give me an example of a time you worked under extreme stress.

375. Tell me about a stressful work situation you have experienced and how you dealt with it.

376. Describe a project or goal that has caused you frustration.

377. Give me an example of a high-pressure situation you have faced this past year and how you resolved it.

378. What kinds of pressures did you feel in your job at _____? Tell me about them. How did you deal with them?

379. Describe situations that you have been under pressure in which you feel you handled well.

**Analysis:** All of these questions are designed to help you understand the candidate's acknowledgement of stress, and determine what types of situations are stress inducing. What you want to hear are details and specifics. Everyone will say they take stress in stride or they try to "get it out of their system," but your job is to uncover what exact strategies the candidate uses to actually accomplish this. It may take some persistent probing, but you really need to assess the candidate's ability to perform under pressure.

Critically examine the coping tactics used and determine how practical they are. Potential interviewees usually anticipate stress questions, so you have to make sure the answer you get is not rehearsed or designed to be impressive. Make sure to ask for a few examples, and the more recent the situation, the more likely the strategy will be used in your workplace.

380. Describe the level of stress in your job and what you do to manage it.

381. What do you do to manage stress?

382. How do you manage stress in your daily work?

383. Describe how you work when you are under pressure.

384. Tell me about the work pace at your previous job?

**Analysis:** These questions are important because they allow you to evaluate whether or not the stress level at your company is more or less intense than what the candidate is used to. It is certainly more difficult to adapt to a more stressful environment, but if the candidate has strong coping strategies, then that will mitigate the situation. Overall, these are fit questions, and you will have to determine if the candidate is suitable for the expected work environment.

385. What are your stress triggers?

386. How do you know when you are under stress?

**Analysis:** Often the first and most important component of dealing with stress is recognizing the early warning signs. Candidates that have developed techniques to counteract the early signs of stress are more likely to effectively combat stress in general. Use these question as lead-ins to the questions that specifically ask for stress-management techniques.

387. Who do you go to for support when you are stressed or under pressure at work?

388. After a difficult day, how do you alleviate your stress?

389. Tell me about a time when you were under stress and a coworker stepped in to help you.

**Analysis:** What you are trying to evaluate here is the extent that the candidate uses external resources to help fight stress. Having outlets for stress relief is very important, and you need to know if the candidate is able to ask for and use the assistance available to him or her. Coworkers and family members are common sources of stress relief but exercise clubs or other hobby groups are often useful as well. Try to determine how varied the candidate's approach to stress management is. The more resources the person employs, the higher the likelihood of success.

390. Tell me about a time when your boss was under a lot of pressure. What did you do?

**Analysis:** Recognizing when others are under pressure is an important element of a strong team player. Using others for support is helpful but offering your own support is invaluable. A candidate who can give and receive support during stressful situations will be a valuable addition to your team.

391. How do you handle the pressure of dealing with a very irate customer, coworker or other person you encounter on the job?

392. Describe a time when you lost your temper.

393. Describe a situation when you had to exercise a significant amount of self-control.

**Analysis:** Professionalism is so hard to maintain when a person is stressed and feeling attacked. Use this type of question to find out how the candidate behaves in the most stressful and uncomfortable situations. What are the things that cause the lid to blow? Don't penalize the person for being honest, and be suspicious of the candidate who replies he or she has never behaved poorly. Focus on what was learned, and use the answers to other stress-related questions to determine the likelihood of it happening again.

394. Describe a recent situation that you just couldn't handle.

**Analysis:** It's important to know a candidate's breaking point before making a hiring decision. Everyone has different levels of coping, and you need to know what situations the candidate just can't deal with, and then make a fit evaluation based on that information. Obviously, the situation should be something that most people who find unbearable. If the candidate expresses an inability to handle a moderate amount of stress, then he or she is not a very strong choice as an employee. As always, evaluate the answer in context and ask for details to make sure you understand the full situation.

395. Describe a time where stress from your personal life threatened to interfere with your work. What did you do?

**Analysis:** Personal and professional lives often mix, but when stress from home affects work, that is a huge problem. Focus your attention on the coping mechanisms and strategies used rather than the personal issue that was causing the stress. You don't want to get into the details of someone's personal life, but you want to know what was done to make the situation bearable at work.

## Application: Stress-Management Skills Questions
### Applicant: Charles Davenport

### Position: Administrative Assistant

Interviewer: "Finally, I want to talk about stress management. Can you tell me what your current workplace is like in terms of stress and pressure?"

Interviewee: "There are times like when quarterly or year-end reports are due or if we have a large deadline to adhere to. Mostly it's pretty casual and we all get along fairly well, so there's not a lot of stress happening between us."

Interviewer: "Can you tell me about a particularly stressful time that you encountered recently and how you handled it?"

Interviewee: "We have a client who has been dealing with

our company for over five years. He wasn't happy about an invoice that was sent to him and I happened to be covering for payroll and accounts that day. Well, this guy is tearing a strip off me on the phone and I can hardly get a word in edge-wise to tell him that I'm not familiar with the invoice but I'll investigate and get back to him. I hadn't ever been talked to like that in a professional capacity so it was all I could do to remain calm. Eventually I was able to get him to agree to wait until I found the invoice and reviewed it. I looked up the invoice and couldn't find anything wrong with the amount but I knew I wasn't going to be able to deal with him when he realized he wasn't going to get any satisfaction, so I explained the situation to the accounting supervisor and he handled the phone call. I'm not even sure how it all ended up because the next day I was back at my own little desk, happy that I didn't have to deal with irate customers in my job."

| | |
|---|---|
| Interviewer: | "Tell me about what triggers stress for you. Use a specific example." |
| | |
| Interviewee: | "Well, that irate customer sure got my dander up. I knew I was getting stressed because my |

heart started beating fast and I could feel my face turning red. I just couldn't believe someone would attack the way he did. Other times when I've been stressed I've started to shake and I could feel the adrenaline rushing inside me. Luckily, I'm an avid jogger so I can get all the tension out on a regular basis that way."

It was pretty obvious from the start of this topic that Charles' ability to handle stress is not that great. His tendency to pass difficult interpersonal issues on to someone else was also evident. The interviewer received answers that confirmed other information she had about Charles and so she chose not to probe further or ask for more details. Interviewing is time-intensive so there is not point in getting more information than you need.

*Know when you've gathered enough detail to make a defensible evaluation of the competency and of the candidate overall.*

# 14

# Summary of Interview Tips

You've followed Charles' interview through 11 competencies. What should be clear is that interviewing is a conversation that is set within pre-identified boundaries. Be open and flexible with the flow of conversation and remember that you are in control. Your goal is to get the information you need, so ask as many follow-up questions as necessary.

Here is a summary of the key tip or technique identified in each section of Charles' interview:

- Use explanatory lead-ins to supplement your behavioral questions, making them relevant to your company and the position.

- Probe, probe and probe some more—you never know what gems of information you will pick up.

- Be on the lookout for areas where the candidate may require some professional development in order to become fully competent in an area.

- Convey neutrality and provide very few feedback cues to the interviewee.

- Consider including opinion and other non-behavioral questions in your structured interview.

- Focus your interview on the five or six competencies most critical for success in the position.

- Continue to probe for specific details that will confirm your opinion about a candidate's competency in a certain area.

- Use each section of the interview questions to confirm or deny previous evaluations you have made.

- Be on the lookout for canned or coached answers and insist on specific, detailed examples for all your behavioral questions.

- Remain flexible throughout the interview and be open to probing for information outside the competency being investigated.

- Know when you've gathered enough detail to make a defensible evaluation of the competency and of the candidate overall.

*What you are assessing with ethics and integrity question the degree of honesty and trustworthiness.*

# 15
# Other Competencies

The interview with Charles covered 11 competencies—double what a typical interview would cover—and there are many more competencies that could have been presented in detail. The next section is a compilation of interview questions for seven more areas of competence that you may choose to evaluate. Use the list of questions to develop your own behaviorally based structured interviews.

## Ethics and Integrity

What you are assessing with ethics and integrity question the degree of honesty and trustworthiness a candidate displays, as well as the likelihood that the person will take responsibility for his or her actions and make decisions that are in the best interest of the company rather than for personal gain.

Use these questions to uncover the following:

- Does the candidate have the character required to avoid

unethical, inappropriate and illegal behavior in the workplace?

- Will this person adhere to his or her values and principles in the face of significant pressure to compromise?

- How easily will this person cave into pressures and act in ways that are not appropriate or even illegal?

- How honest is the candidate?

- Is this person loyal?

- Is this person reliable?

- Does this person respect confidentiality?

## Ethics and Integrity Questions

396. Tell me about your level of integrity.

397. What will your references tell me about your integrity?

398. Describe a politically sensitive situation that you were in and how you handled the situation.

399. Tell me about a time when you knew you made a mistake but there was little chance of anyone else finding out. How did you handle the mistake and what was the resolution?

400. Tell me about a time when you bypassed your supervisor and went to your supervisor's supervisor to handle a situation.

401. Tell me about a situation that illustrates your ability to exercise good judgment.

402. Describe a situation where you had to keep information confidential.

403. Describe a situation in which you promised more than you could deliver. How did you handle it?

404. Give me an example of time when you chose to be completely honest, even when doing so was risky and potentially damaging for you.

405. Tell me about a time when you believe someone broke unwritten rules or violated acceptable business behavior. What was your role and what happened?

406. Can you tell me about a situation when you had to bend the rules to get the job done?

407. Tell me about a time when someone challenged your integrity. How did you handle it?

408. Describe a recent moral or ethical dilemma you have encountered.

409. Recall for me a time when you were aware that a fellow employee did something inappropriate, unethical or illegal? What did you do?

410. Explain to me a situation where you withheld information from your supervisor. What was the reason and the outcome?

411. Tell me about a time you may have taken credit for someone else's work.

412. Tell me about a time when you did the bulk of the work for a team assignment. How did you handle the team recognition versus personal recognition?

413. Describe the types of personal activities you do on work time.

414. If you knew your company was committing a serious legal violation, what would you do?

415. Have you ever resigned from a position because you felt company ethics were not being adhered to? Tell me about the situation.

416. Tell me about a time when honesty was not the best policy.

417. On what occasions have you been tempted to lie?

418. Describe for me a time when your boss gave you an order that violated company policy.

419. Have you ever been fired? Tell me about it.

420. Tell me about a specific time when you had to handle a tough problem which challenged fairness or ethical issues.

421. Discuss a time when your integrity was challenged. How did you handle it?

422. Tell me about a time when you experienced personal loss or disadvantage for doing what was right. How did you react?

423. Tell me about a situation when you were asked to do something that you thought was a conflict of interest. How did you deal with the situation?

424. Please relate for me an experience where you found out a coworker was taking work supplies for personal use. What did you do?

425. Have you ever intervened on behalf of an employee who was not being treated fairly? Tell me about it.

# 16

# Work Ethics and Professionalism

These questions assess the likelihood that the candidate will perform at high levels of productivity long after the initial "best first impression" phase is over. What you are looking for is a candidate who performs his or her work with professionalism and makes decisions that are in the best interest of the company. Attributes addressed include:

- Accountability

- Commitment to quality

- Composure

- Dedication

- Dependability

- Diligence

- Positive attitude

- Responsibility

## Work Ethic and Professionalism Questions

426. Tell me about a last-minute assignment that put you under a short deadline. How did you accomplish the task on time? How accurate was your end result?

427. After being given an assignment, how do you prepare to "tackle" the assignment?

428. Tell me about a time when you were sick or had other personal commitments that got in the way of completing an assignment on time.

429. What is the best job you have ever done on an assignment? What do you use as your own personal benchmark for success?

430. Tell me about a time that you exceeded a coworker's or boss's expectations.

431. It is thirty minutes before the end of the official workday. You have just finished a large project. What do you do in those last thirty minutes of the day?

432. Is there a particular experience that stands out as one you never want to repeat because you did not meet

your normal standards of performance? Explain the situation.

433. Tell me about a time when you were asked to complete a task that you didn't know anything about. How did you complete the task? What was the result?

434. Describe a time when you went above and beyond the call of duty.

435. Recall for me a time when you made a personal sacrifice in order to help a coworker meet his or her deadline or job responsibility.

436. Tell me about a time when you were late or absent to work. How did you communicate that to your supervisor? How many workdays have you missed in the last year?

437. Tell me about the most challenging task you have ever been faced with. What did you do to meet that challenge?

438. Would you describe yourself as someone who goes the extra mile? Tell me why.

439. Would you describe yourself as task-oriented or concept-oriented? Tell me about it.

440. Describe for me a time when you filled in for someone who had different or lower-level responsibilities than your own?

441. Recall for me the last opportunity you took to keep informed or up to date professionally.

442. Describe something you have done that demonstrated professionalism.

443. Tell me about your last performance review. What areas were exemplary and what areas needed improvement?

444. Tell me how you compose yourself after things have not gone as planned or expected.

445. Give me an example of how determined you are.

446. Has anyone ever criticized your work? If so, how did you handle it?

447. Give me an example of how you saw a project through despite numerous obstacles.

448. Tell me about one of the most difficult work experiences you have ever had.

449. Tell me about a time when your diplomacy skills were really put to the test.

450. Tell me about a time when you felt you did not perform to expectations.

*Some workplaces are more structured than others, but there is always a fundamental set of rules and regulations that apply.*

# 17
## Compliance

All workplaces operate within a set of rules. Some workplaces are more structured than others, but there is always a fundamental set of rules and regulations that apply. Some rules are explicit and others may be more cultural or "that's the way it's done around here." The compliance section allows you to determine a candidate's respect for and adherence to these rules. Your job is to assess the following:

- Ability to follow established guidelines.

- Understand and respect for policies and procedures.

- Recognition of the importance of consistency.

- Level of impulsive behavior.

- Ability to stick to a routine.

## Compliance Questions

451. Give a specific example of a policy you conformed to with which you did not agree.

452. Tell me about a recent business problem you solved. How did you utilize organizational structure (policies, systems, etc.) to solve the problem?

453. Tell me about a time when you knowingly disregarded an organizational policy. Why did you choose to disregard the policy? What happened?

454. Tell me about a time your organization was unable to keep a commitment you made. What happened?

455. Give me an example of a time when you made a decision only to find out later that it was rejected. Why was it rejected? Why, do you think, was it not approved through your systems?

456. Give me an example of a time when a company policy or action hurt people. What, if anything, did you do to mitigate the negative consequences to people?

457. Recall for me a time when a coworker violated a company policy. What was your reaction and what was the outcome?

458. What is the farthest you have to bend your standards in order to succeed?

459. Tell me about a time when you had to follow a superior's orders when you did not agree with them.

460. Describe a time when you were given specific procedures to complete your job but knew that if you skipped some of the formalities, you could complete your job more quickly. What did you do?

461. Tell me about a time when you discovered a quality issue. What did you do to address the problem?

462. Recall for me a time when you ignored a safety violation or broke a safety rule in the name of improved efficiency.

*Adaptability is how people cope with continuous change.*

# 18
# Adaptability

I'm sure you have heard that "the only constant is change."
Adaptability is how people cope with continuous change. Some
organizations change rapidly and frequently, while others are
less intense. For those companies where change is a permanent
fixture, assessing a candidate's level of flexibility and
adaptability is crucial.

Questions within this area of competency are designed for you
to assess a candidate's ability to deal with the following
situations:

- Ambiguity

- Constraints

- Rapid change

- Frustration

- Shifting priorities

- Multiple demands

- Frustrating circumstances

- Identifying other's needs

- Putting other's needs first

## Adaptability Questions

463. What do you do when your schedule is suddenly interrupted? Provide an example.

464. Describe a time you had to be flexible in planning a workload.

465. Describe a time when you were working on a project that suddenly changed in mid-stream.

466. Tell me about a situation when you had to adjust quickly to change in organizational/departmental or team priorities. How did the change affect you?

467. Tell of some situations in which you have had to adjust quickly to changes over which you had no control. What was the impact of the change on you?

468. How was your transition from high school to college? Did you face any particular problems?

469. Tell me about a time that it was crucial for you to remain focused on the task at hand but you kept getting interrupted. What did you do to ensure your focus was where it needed to be?

470. Tell me about a time when you changed your priorities to meet others' expectations.

471. Describe a time when you altered your own behavior to fit the situation.

472. Tell me about a time when you had to change your point of view or your plans to take into account new information or changing priorities.

473. Tell me about a time when you worked with a person who did things very differently from you. How did you get the job done?

474. By providing examples, demonstrate that you can adapt to a wide variety of people, situations and/or environments.

475. Tell me about a time when you had to adjust to a classmate's or colleague's working style in order to

complete a project or achieve your objectives.

476. Has your job ever changed because of re-organization? Please explain how you handled the situation.

477. Recall a major change you went through at work. How did you handle it?

478. Describe a change you have made to your work environment.

479. Tell me about a time you had to change your work priorities to respond to other company matters.

480. Can you give me an example of how you helped others effectively handle a changing environment?

481. Tell me about a time when rapid change created a problem for you.

482. Tell me about a time when you changed your priorities to meet others' needs.

483. Tell me about a time when you had to change your plans to take into account new information.

484. Describe a time when you adapted guidelines or procedures in order to get the job done.

485. Tell me about a time when you adjusted to a colleague's practice or procedure because it was proven to be a more effective method.

486. Describe a time when you identified and communicated a need for change in your department or organization. What did you do?

487. Describe a time when you changed a long-term strategy to address a new situation.

488. Tell me about a time you had to adapt to a new supervisor or manager. What did you do?

489. What do you do when your schedule is suddenly interrupted? Give a specific example.

490. Have you ever had an experience where you found it

impossible to adapt to a changing circumstance? Tell me about it.

491. Tell me about a time you may have been asked to completely change jobs in order to stay employed with your company.

492. Tell me about a time you had to be flexible in arranging your work schedule and your personal life.

# 19
# Leadership

Not all positions require formal leadership, but the characteristics of effective leaders are often desirable across a variety of positions. The important issue for you to uncover is the candidate's personal beliefs around what an effective leader does and how he or she goes about doing it. Whether the position is management or staff, you need to evaluate the candidate's ability to motivate and positively influence others in the workplace.

Leadership questions focus on the following characteristics:

- Open and accessible communicator

- Team player

- Values diversity

- Fosters creativity

- Shares information and expectations

- Welcomes ideas

- Values all contributions

- Facilitates participation

- Acknowledges mistakes

- Demonstrates enthusiasm

- Offers feedback

- Acts as a role model

- Empowers others

## Leadership Questions

493. Describe your management philosophy and management style. Provide examples.

494. What leadership positions have you held? Describe your leadership style.

495. Tell me about a time when you coached someone to help them improve their skills or job performance. What did you do?

496. Describe a time when you provided feedback to someone about his or her performance.

497. Describe a situation where you helped someone establish his or her objectives.

498. Give me an example of a time when you recognized that a member of your team had a performance difficulty/deficiency. What did you do?

499. Please describe a situation in which you were responsible for organizing the training of other people, in addition to being responsible for your own daily tasks.

500. Tell me about a time when you prepared for and led an important meeting.

501. Were you ever responsible for the outcome of someone else's efforts? Please tell me about it.

502. Tell me about the time you demonstrated your best leadership abilities.

503. Give me an example of your leadership style.

504. Give me an example of a situation where you took charge.

505. Tell me about the characteristics that you demonstrate

that make you a good leader. Give me an example where you used that characteristic.

506. What are three effective leadership qualities you think are important? How have you demonstrated these qualities in your past/current position?

507. Can you tell me about a time when you pushed your staff to complete a project on time even though the outcome was less than optimal?

508. Describe a time when you tried to persuade another person to do something that he or she was not very willing to do.

509. Provide an example of a time when you had to persuade people to do something that they didn't want to do.

510. What is the toughest group that you have had to get cooperation from? Describe how you handled it. What was the outcome?

511. Have you ever been a member of a group where two of the members did not work well together? What did you

do to help them get along?

512. Tell me about a time when you coached someone to success on a task or project.

513. Tell me about a team project when you had to take the lead or take charge of the project? What did you do? How did you do it? What was the result?

514. Describe a leadership role of yours. Why did you commit your time to it? How did you feel about it?

515. What is the toughest group that you have had to get cooperation from? What were the obstacles? How did you handle the situation? What were the reactions of the group members? What was the end result?

516. Have you ever had difficulty getting others to accept your ideas? What was your approach? Did it work?

517. Tell me about a time when you delegated a project effectively.

518. Of the people you have encountered or know about in

public positions of leadership, who do you look to as a role model and why?

519. Tell me about a situation in which you supervised someone whose performance was substandard.

520. Describe a situation where you helped motivate someone to improve his or her performance.

521. Tell me about a time when you had to conduct a particularly difficult employee counseling or corrective session. How did you prepare for the session? Did you delay having it? How long?

522. Tell me about a time when an employee you supervised disagreed with you about a work issue and suggested an alternate way the issue might be addressed. How did you handle that?

523. Give me an example of a leadership experience you have had.

524. When have you felt most comfortable as a leader?

525. How do you ensure that your team is working effectively?

526. How do you reward employees?

527. What techniques do you use to motivate others?

528. Have you patterned your management style after someone in particular? Tell me about it.

529. Describe a situation where you contributed to a team effort when you were not the leader.

530. Describe a time when you had to change your leadership style.

531. How have you demonstrated leadership by example?

532. What methods do you use as a leader to foster open communication?

533. What event made you least proud to be a leader?

534. What steps have you had to take in disciplining an employee or group member?

535. Have you ever had to overcome weaknesses as a manager? If so, how did you overcome them?

536. How do you handle an employee who is not doing his or her work correctly?

537. Tell me about some of the people who have become successful as a result of your management. What was your role in their development?

538. What was your most recent mistake leading a team, and how did you repair the situation?

539. Describe a situation that required you to inspire excitement and enthusiasm in your team or direct staff.

# 20
# Creativity

Creativity is not limited to artistic people. Creativity can be found in one's ability to generate creative or original solutions to problems and find innovative ways to solve old problems. Creativity is a valuable competency because it demonstrates an ability to think beyond a job description and see how a role impacts coworkers, supervisors and the overall performance of the company.

The types of questions you should ask yourself when approaching creativity questions are:

- Is this person capable of bringing fresh and inventive ideas to light?

- Will this person bring original thinking to the company?

- Is the person's creativity tempered with practicality?

- Has this person improved processes?

- Does this person challenge the "that's the way it has always been done" mentality?

## Creativity Questions

540. Describe something you have done that was new and different for your organization that improved performance and/or productivity.

541. Tell me about a time when you identified a new, unusual or different approach for addressing a problem or task.

542. Tell me about a recent problem in which old solutions wouldn't work. How did you solve the problem?

543. Describe for me the most innovative idea or approach that you were able to implement successfully on the job.

544. Tell me about a time when an idea you brought to fruition did not live up to your expectations.

545. Describe a situation in which you took a creative approach to finding the resources needed to accomplish a goal.

546. Tell me about a time when you created a new process or program that was considered risky. What was the situation and what did you do?

547. Describe the most significant or creative presentation/idea that you developed/implemented.

548. When was the last time you thought "outside the box" and how did you do it? Why?

549. Tell me about a problem that you've solved in a unique or unusual way. What was the outcome? Were you happy or satisfied with it?

550. Give me an example of when someone brought you a new idea that was odd or unusual. What did you do?

551. Please describe a situation where you used your creativity to solve a problem.

552. Tell me about a time when your innovative approach convinced someone to try something new.

553. Did you ever develop a creative solution to a problem? Tell me about it.

554. Give an example of a time when you had to teach someone a skill and how you went about it.

555. Are you the type of person who likes to "try new things" or "stay with regular routines"? Give an example.

556. What would you regard as being the most creative activity you have engaged in? Did it bring you recognition, financial reward or personal satisfaction?

557. What would you say has been the most creative accomplishment in your last position? Be specific.

558. Are you an innovator? Provide examples.

559. Tell me about a technical problem you have solved.

560. Have you ever been recognized or rewarded for your creativity? Tell me about it?

561. Can you tell me about a non-artistic situation or problem which required creativity?

562. What types of creative work give you the most satisfaction?

563. Give an example of how you have had to overcome an obstacle in a creative way.

564. Tell me about a time an existing process was not working and you found a solution.

565. Tell me about an improvement you personally initiated.

566. Describe a time when you came up with a solution when others couldn't.

567. Describe how you feel when you find solutions to problems that others did not recognize?

568. Describe an instance when you had to think on your feet to extricate yourself from a difficult situation.

569. Describe an idea that was implemented successfully because of the efforts you made.

570. Have you found any ways to make your job easier or more rewarding? Describe them.

571. Tell me about a time your company was facing a challenge and you came up with an innovative solution.

# 21
# Skill-Based
# Behavioral Questions

The final area of competency questions relates to specific skills, abilities and qualifications. In addition to "soft" skills that are required for general job success, there are "hard" skills that are required in order to perform specific jobs. Many of the skill-based competencies can be sufficiently evaluated from information on the résumé. There are instances, though, when you need or want to confirm the level of expertise a candidate claims to bring to the table. In those instances, skill-based questions provide an excellent and efficient method.

Some employers choose to conduct pre-employment tests to evaluate qualification and skill level, but time and resource constraints often mean that those competencies are evaluated during the structured interview process.

Use and adapt the following skill-based competency questions for your specific workplace and functional position:

## Skill = Computers

572. At what computer programs are you proficient?

573. Tell me about the types of activities for which you use your computer.

574. What was the most complex problem you used your computer to help you solve?

575. Explain to me the process you went through to design your last database.

576. When you have a task that requires analyzing large amount of data, what computer programs or resources do you use to assist you?

577. What percentage of your time at work is spent working on a computer?

578. Describe a recent project where you used the Internet as a valuable resource tool.

579. What is your experience level with e-mail and Intranets?

580. Tell me about your experience in network administration.

581. Tell me about a time when you assisted someone else with a computer-related problem.

582. With what programming languages are you proficient?

583. Tell me about the most challenging application you worked on.

584. What techniques and tools do you use to ensure that a new application is as user-friendly as possible?

585. What steps do you use to check the accuracy of your code? Use a specific example.

586. Describe for me the last problem involving computer hardware that you solved.

587. What are the various tools and measures that can be implemented to secure data?

588. Recall for me a time when you were responsible for securing electronic data. How did you determine what needed to be done and what was the result?

## Skill = Accounting

589. Tell me about your experience with accounts receivable.

590. Explain for me an experience you had involving collections.

591. What process do you go though to prepare a bill for services?

592. Tell me about your experience with accounts payable.

593. Recall for me a time when you discovered a discrepancy in an invoice. What did you do and what was the result?

594. Describe the types of financial reports you have prepared.

595. Describe your experiences with cash flow analysis

596. How familiar are you with variance analyses?

597. What experience do you have with cost accounting? What systems have you worked with?

598. Explain the depth of your accounting responsibility at your current job.

599. Describe for me your experience with budgeting.

600. What experience do you have with tax accounting?

601. How involved have you been in the auditing process at your company?

602. Recall for me what you did the last time your figures did not balance?

603. What is our experience with setting up accounting systems?

604. What role do you play in monitoring the accuracy of accounts?

## Skill = Teaching

605. Describe a situation where you had to "think on your feet" to handle an emerging unexpected situation.

606. What specific approaches or ideas do you have for dealing with at-risk students?

607. What strategies do you use to improve reading skills of students who are far below grade level?

608. Describe the process you would use to deal with a student who was disrupting the class.

609. Describe the parts of your portfolio that best indicate your teaching style and beliefs.

610. What provisions do you make for meeting the range of

skills and needs commonly present in a classroom?

611. Describe a team project you have done and your role.

612. What steps have you taken prior to parent-teacher conference to ensure its success?

613. Describe your experiences working with a diverse student body.

614. Explain a difficult situation, how you handled it, what you learned from it, and what would you do differently now.

## Skill = Customer Service

615. Is the customer always right?

616. Tell me about a situation with a very demanding customer that you handled well.

617. Tell me about a situation with a very demanding customer that you handled poorly. What went wrong? What would you do differently?

618. Recall for me a time when you provided superb customer service.

619. Give me an example of a recognition (formal or informal) you received for quality service.

620. When you move to a new company, how have you become proficient with the company's products and services?

621. Tell me about how you handled a dissatisfied customer.

622. Describe the last time a customer interrupted you when you were in the middle of completing an assignment for your boss. What did you do?

623. Recall for me a time when a customer was abusive with you. What did you do? What was the outcome?

624. What experience do you have with developing customer surveys or other feedback tools?

625. Describe for me a time when you noticed a coworker

having difficulty with a customer. What did you do? What was the outcome?

## Skill = Supervision

626. Describe your supervisory experience.

627. In your role as supervisor, what had been your greatest challenge?

628. What one supervisory experience stands out as the most rewarding?

629. Tell me about a time when your role as supervisor was least enjoyable.

630. Describe for me the last conflict between two of your employees that you got personally involved in. What was the situation and result?

631. In your role as supervisor, when have you felt it necessary to involve your boss in a decision or problem? What was the outcome?

632. What is the most difficult aspect of supervision?

633. Tell me about a time when you had to delegate supervisory responsibility to one of your employees. How did you decide who was given authority? What was the reaction?

634. Tell me about the most difficult personal problem you helped an employee work through.

635. Describe for me a time when you were part of the decision to fire an employee.

636. What is your method of employee correction or discipline? Provide examples.

637. Have you ever been involved with discrimination or harassment issues? Tell me about your role and what the final outcome was.

638. Recall for me a time when you had to deal with excessive absenteeism. What did you do? What was the result?

## Skill = General Office

639. How many words do you type per minute?

640. With is your experience with dictation?

641. What types of reports and documents have you been responsible for preparing?

642. Describe for me a time when you had an unexpected office visitor. What did you do?

643. Recall for me a time when there were many people waiting for appointments. What did you do and what was the result?

644. Tell me about a time when you were given competing directions from two people. How did you determine what to do?

645. Describe a time when you were responsible for handling your boss's schedule. What strategies do you use to keep him or her informed?

646. Tell me about a time your boss got frustrated or short with you. How did you react? What was the outcome?

647. What is the best experience you have had as an office assistant?

648. Tell me about a time when you let your boss down?
What happened? What would you do differently?

649. How do you determine the best form of communication? For instance, when do you use a letter versus a memo or e-mail versus a notice on the bulletin board?

650. What types of business documents are you responsible for preparing?

651. Walk me through your process to make sure all correspondence is accurate?

## Skill = Sales

652. Is your current compensation commission or salary or a combination? What do you like best and least about the compensation structure?

653. Tell me about a time when you spent a great deal of time with a customer and you did not get the sale.

654. Recall for me a time when a coworker snatched a sale from under you. What did you do? What was the outcome?

655. What steps do you take to overcome a prospect's sales resistance? Use an example.

656. Tell me about the longest sale you ever completed? Why did it take so long? What could you have done differently?

657. Tell me about your closing technique. Provide a few examples.

658. Tell me about a time when you used deception in order to finalize a sale.

659. Recall for me the largest sale you lost? What happened? What did you learn from the experience?

660. What is your strategy for dealing with buyer's remorse? Use an example.

661. Where do you generate your best leads?

662. Tell me about your most loyal customer.

663. Tell me about a time when you failed to meet your sales goal. What went wrong?

664. Tell me about a time when your actual sales far exceeded your projected sales. What contributed most to your success?

665. What percentage of your sales comes from current customers and how much comes from new leads?

666. Describe for me the most outrageous thing you did to close a sale.

## Skill = Marketing

667. Describe for me your most successful marketing plan.

668. Describe for me your least successful marketing plan.

669. How do you see marketing differentiates from sales?

670. To what extent are you responsible for developing and monitoring a marketing plan. Use an example.

671. Tell me about a time when you identified a growth market and provided a strategy to move into that market.

672. What sorts of variables do you consider before developing a marketing plan?

673. Tell me about the last marketing plan you put together.

674. Recall for me the best marketing strategy you put together.

675. Recall a time when you failed to foresee a significant consequence of your marketing plan. What happened? What would you do differently?

676. Describe your approach to market research.

677. What have you done to familiarize yourself with new industries and emerging markets?

678. Tell me about a promotion campaign you were directly involved in.

679. Describe your involvement with focus groups and other direct means of gathering market information.

680. Tell me about a success you experienced in niche marketing.

## Skill = Human Service

681. What experiences and unique perspectives do you bring to this agency?

682. Tell me about specific individuals you worked with that had multiple difficulties. How did you manage the case? What was the outcome?

683. What inspired you to choose a career in human services?

684. What kind of experience have you had with different populations (i.e., women, youth, terminally ill, etc.)? Use examples.

685. Explain why you are interested in working with our specific client population.

686. What was the most difficult case you worked on?

687. Tell me about a time when you and other human service professionals disagreed on the best treatment of a mutual client. How did you handle the situation? What was the outcome?

688. Tell me about the one case that you will never forget? What made it unforgettable?

690. Explain the specific strategies and techniques you use in crisis-intervention work.

691. Tell me about a situation in which you crossed your professional boundaries? What happened?

692. Recall for me the most frustrating individual you worked with. What made the situation so frustrating and what was the end result?

693. Tell me about a time when you declined to work with an individual. How did you make your decision?

694. How have you dealt with a lack of professional resources needed to do your job?

695. What is the most recent professional development activity you participated in?

696. Tell me about a time when you suffered from professional burnout. How did you cope? What was the end result?

# 22
# Final Words

Well, you've made it to the end of the questions but your job has just begun. Take the time to analyze the position you are attempting to fill. After you have decided which competencies to evaluate, go through each section and choose the questions that are most applicable to your workplace. Some will work as is and others will need a bit of modification. After reading though and becoming familiar with the behavioral interview approach, you will be confident to develop your own questions tailored specifically for each position in your company.

## Follow This Succinct Recipe for Interviewing Success

1. Keep in mind the Golden Rule of behavioral interviewing

   **The Best Predictor of Future Behavior is Past Behavior**

2. Ask yourself with every question:

Did the candidate's answer give me specific details about actions, responses and outcomes?

3.    (a) If your answer is "yes," then you have what you need to make an evaluation.

(b) If your answer is "no," then you need to probe further.

# 23
# Summary List of Competencies

| Competency | Definition |
| --- | --- |
| Accountability | Takes personal responsibility for outcomes. |
| Adapting to Change | Is very flexible and adaptable; copes well with change. |
| Business Mindedness | Understands the nature of the company's business and how his or her own role affects the bottom line. |
| Communication | Expresses oneself well verbally. |

| **Competency** (continued) | **Definition** (continued) |
|---|---|
| Conflict Management | Finds common ground to resolve issues. |
| Cooperation and Collaboration | Works well with others to achieve business and team goals. |
| Creating and Communicating Vision | Makes real to everyone inspiring an vision. |
| Critical Thinking | Develops solutions to business problems. |
| Customer Focus | Concentrates on customers' best interests. |
| Dealing with Ambiguity | Embraces change and can comfortably handle risk and uncertainty. |
| Detail-Oriented | Is meticulous and precise in approach; quality-conscious and thorough. |

| **Competency** (continued) | **Definition** (continued) |
|---|---|
| Development | Improves oneself or others professionally. |
| Drive for Results | Consistently meets/exceeds goals; is action-oriented and passionate about the work; seizes opportunities. |
| Functional Knowledge | Well-developed knowledge of own functional area of expertise. |
| Influencing Others | Negotiates "win-win" outcomes in tough situations. |
| Initiative | Demonstrates self-motivation through action. |
| Innovation | Generates creative new ideas. |
| Integrity/Ethical Behavior | Is trustworthy and demonstrates strong personal and professional values. |

| **Competency** (continued) | **Definition** (continued) |
|---|---|
| Interpersonal Skills | Relates well to all kinds of people at all levels within and outside the organization. |
| Leadership Potential | Motivates and inspires others. |
| Learning Attitude | Pursues learning with drive and vigor. |
| Maintaining Composure/Flexibility | Is tolerant of people and processes, and can deal well with change and new information. |
| Management Skills | Sets employee goals; coaches and monitors performance. |
| Managerial Courage | Doesn't hold back; makes tough decisions even when those decisions are unpopular. |
| Motivating Others | Empowers others to succeed. |

| **Competency** (continued) | **Definition** (continued) |
|---|---|
| Planning and Organizing | Uses time and resources efficiently to accomplish work objectives. |
| Priority and Goal Setting | Quickly discovers the source of problems and generates thoughtful, effective solutions. |
| Problem Solving | Takes control of challenging projects with foresight and implementation focus. |
| Project Planning | Focuses effort on most important goals and objectives. |
| Risk Taking | Takes well-calculated business risks, learning from mistakes and false starts. |
| Service Orientation | Committed to meeting and exceeding customer expectations. |

| **Competency** (continued) | **Definition** (continued) |
|---|---|
| Strategic Agility | Is visionary; anticipates future consequences and trends. |
| Teamwork | Works well with others to achieve shared goals. |
| Technical Knowledge and Proficiency | Accurately and consistently applies technical principles and practice to situations on the job. |
| Time Management | Uses time effectively and efficiently, concentrating efforts on most important priorities. |
| Works Independently | High degree of comfort operating autonomously. |

# Index

Accountability 277

Accounting 260

Adaptability 237, 238

Adapting to change 277

Ambiguity 278

Analytical ability 123

Analytical skills 124, 132

Analyze 128, 275

Asking questions 44

Assertiveness 73

Behavioral 257, 275

Business-mindedness 277

Career objectives 26

Communicating vision 278

Communication 43, 50, 52, 55, 56, 57, 170, 277

Communication skills 61

Competency 9, 11, 43, 217, 221, 237, 277, 282

Compliance 233

Computers 258

Confidence 138

Conflict management 278

Conflict resolution 67, 79, 85

Cooperation 278

Creativity 251, 252

Critical thinking 278

Cultural differences 96

Customer service 91, 102, 263, 278

Deadlines 170

Decision making 137, 139, 142, 144, 146

Detail-oriented 278

Detecting inconsistencies 45

Development 279

Effective listening 44

Empathy 91, 92, 94, 103

Ethical behavior 279

Ethics 221, 222

Evaluate 185, 276

Flexibility 280

General office 266

Get-to-know-you questions 20

Goal setting 281

Honest 221

Human service 272

Influencing 279

Initiative 193, 194, 196, 200, 279

Innovation 279

Integrity 221, 222, 279

Interpersonal skills 67, 78, 85, 280

Interview 15, 16, 18, 19, 30, 35, 219

Interview tips 217

Interviewing success 275

Job performance 25

Judgment 138

Knowledge 279

Leadership 243, 244, 280

Learning 280

Listen 53, 54, 70

Maintaining contact 45

Management skills 280

Managerial courage 280

Managing 28

Marketing 270

Motivation 177, 178, 183, 187

Organization 163, 164, 173, 281

Paraphrasing 45

Persistence 138

Planning 281

Presentation 58, 59

Priority 281

Probe 36, 37, 39, 40, 127, 276

Problem solving 107, 108, 110, 115, 117, 281

Professional 218

Professionalism 213, 227, 228, 230

Proficiency 282

Responsibility 221

Results 279

Risk 141, 281

Sales 268

Scholastic experience 23

Self-confidence 138

Self-evaluation 27

Service 91

Service orientation 97, 103, 281

Skill 258, 260, 262, 263, 265, 266, 268, 270, 272

Skill-based 257

Small talk 17, 19

Strategic agility 282

Stress 170

Stress management 207, 208, 214

Successful interview 9

Summarizing 45

Supervision 265

Teaching 262

Teamwork 149, 150, 152, 158, 282

Time management 282

Verbal communication 49

Work ethic 227, 228

Work history 21

Written communication 46

## MORE GREAT TITLES FROM ATLANTIC PUBLISHING

**Item # 365-01 • $24.95**
**288 Pages**
**ISBN 0-910627-51-7**

# 365 WAYS TO MOTIVATE AND REWARD YOUR EMPLOYEES EVERY DAY—WITH LITTLE OR NO MONEY

This book is packed with hundreds of simple and inexpensive ways to motivate, challenge and reward your employees. Employees today need constant re-enforcement and recognition—and here's how to do it. You will find real-life, proven examples and case studies from actual companies that you can put to use immediately. You can use this book daily to boost morale, productivity and profits. This is your opportunity to build an organization that people love to work at with these quick, effective, humorous, innovative and fun solutions to employee challenges. Make your business a happy place to work, and reap the benefits.

# SUPERIOR CUSTOMER SERVICE: HOW TO KEEP CUSTOMERS RACING BACK TO YOUR BUSINESS—TIME-TESTED EXAMPLES FROM LEADING COMPANIES

This book details how to care for customers and how to make superior service happen, and keep customers coming back to your store or Web site. This book is a ready-made, in-house training workshop and step-by-step manual for creating superior customer service in an ever-competitive business environment. Learn from successful companies what works and what doesn't.

**Item # SCS-01 • $19.95**
**288 Pages**
**ISBN 0-910627-52-5**

To order call toll-free 800-814-1132
or visit www.atlantic-pub.com

# MORE GREAT TITLES FROM ATLANTIC PUBLISHING

Item # HBS-01 • $24.95
288 Pages
ISBN 0-910627-53-3

# HOW TO BUY AND/OR SELL A SMALL BUSINESS FOR MAXIMUM PROFIT – A STEP-BY-STEP GUIDE

This book provides a road map of suggestions, insights and techniques for both buyers and sellers. It covers the entire selling process step by step. Topics covered include: finding and evaluating a business to buy and/or sell; how to value a business; raising the necessary capital; evaluating a business's financial condition using discounted cash flow, excess earnings, asset value, and income capitalization; financing; negotiating and structuring the final deal; brokers; leveraged buyouts; definitive agreements; due diligence; letters of intent; tax concerns; and contracts.

# EBAY INCOME: HOW ANYONE OF ANY AGE, LOCATION AND/OR BACKGROUND CAN BUILD A HIGHLY PROFITABLE ONLINE BUSINESS WITH EBAY

Item # EBY-01 • $24.95
288 Pages
ISBN 0-910627-58-4

There are businesses earning $1 million a year selling products on eBay today. This new book will arm you with the proper knowledge and insider secrets. It starts with a complete overview of how eBay works. Then the book will guide you through the whole process of creating the auction and auction strategies, photography, writing copy, text and formatting, managing auctions, shipping, collecting payments, registering, About Me page, sources for merchandise, multiple sales, programming tricks, PayPal, accounting, creating marketing, merchandising, managing e-mail lists, taxes and sales tax, and everything you will ever need to get started making money on eBay.

# HOW TO COMMUNICATE WITH YOUR SPANISH & ASIAN EMPLOYEES: A TRANSLATION GUIDE FOR SMALL-BUSINESS OWNERS

**Item # CSA-02 • $39.95**
**288 Pages**
**ISBN 0910627-39-8**

The purpose of this book is to help small-business owners and employers learn to communicate with employees whose mother tongue is not English. This two-part handbook is applicable for use in an office environment, the food service and hospitality industry or retail arena. The first part of this manual is intended to be a resource guide for employers. The second part of this book is a glossary and phrase book designed to help your employees learn basic English conversation and language they may encounter in the workplace. The extensive glossary includes definitions of common Spanish and Chinese words arranged by categories. Includes a CD-ROM employee handbook in Spanish and Chinese.

# HOW TO USE THE INTERNET TO ADVERTISE, PROMOTE AND MARKET YOUR BUSINESS OR WEB SITE WITH LITTLE OR NO MONEY

**Item # HIA-01 • $24.95**
**288 Pages**
**ISBN 910627-57-6**

This book presents a comprehensive, hands-on, step-by-step guide for increasing Web site traffic and traditional store traffic by using hundreds of proven tips, tools and techniques. Learn how to target more customers to your business and optimize your Web site from a marketing perspective. You will learn to target your campaign, generate free advertising, search-engine strategies, learn the inside secrets of e-mail marketing, how to build Web communities, co-branding, auto-responders, Google advertising, banner advertising, eBay store fronts, and much more.

To order call toll-free **800-814-1132**
or visit www.atlantic-pub.com

## MORE GREAT TITLES FROM ATLANTIC PUBLISHING

**Item # TFH-01**
**$39.95 • 288 Pages**

# THE FRANCHISE HANDBOOK: A COMPLETE GUIDE TO ALL ASPECTS OF BUYING, SELLING OR INVESTING IN A FRANCHISE

This brand new, comprehensive "bible" details everything you need to know about this popular method to business ownership or business expansion. This book will be a great resource for both prospective franchisees and franchisors as it explains in detail what the franchise system entails and the precise benefits it offers to both parties.

# HOW TO GET THE FINANCING FOR YOUR NEW SMALL BUSINESS: INNOVATIVE SOLUTIONS FROM THE EXPERTS WHO DO IT EVERY DAY

This book will provide you with a road map to securing financing. The book goes into traditional financing methods and assists the reader in setting up proper financial statements and a proper business plan. It details the differences between debt and equity financing and how and why to use each, and much more.

**Item # HGF-01**
**$39.95 • 288 Pages**

**Item # GBP-01**
**$39.95 • 288 Pages**

# HOW TO WRITE A GREAT BUSINESS PLAN FOR YOUR SMALL BUSINESS IN 60 MINUTES OR LESS

This book and companion CD-ROM will demonstrate how to construct a current and pro-forma balance sheet, an income statement and a cash flow analysis. You will learn to allocate resources properly, handle unforeseen complications, and make good business decisions. The CD-ROM file (written in Microsoft Word) allows you to simply plug in your own information while providing specific and organized information about your company.

To order call toll-free **800-814-1132**
or visit www.atlantic-pub.com